How to Run for Local Office

A complete, step-by-step guide that will take you through the entire process of running and winning a local election.

Robert J. Thomas

**First Edition
Second Printing**

R & T Enterprise, Inc., Westland, Michigan

Copyright © 1999 by Robert J. Thomas

Published by R&T Enterprise, Inc. Printed and bound in the United States by BookCrafters of Chelsea, Michigan.

Publisher's Cataloging-in-Publication
(Provided by Quality Books, Inc.)

Thomas, Robert J., 1950-
    How to run for local office / by Robert J.
Thomas. -- 1st ed.
    p. cm.
    LCCN: 98-92286
    ISBN: 0-9668304-0-7

    1. Electioneering--United States--Handbooks, manuals, etc. 2. Campaign management--United States--Handbooks, manuals, etc.   I. Title.

JK2283.T46 1999   324.7'0973
                        QBI99-95

To Jill

I would not be the person I am today without your love and support. There are no words that can express my undying gratitude to you for the love and faith you have shown me. If I am lucky enough to live to be one hundred years old, my only wish is that I will spend each and every one of them with you by my side.

You had faith in me when others didn't.

You supported me when others wouldn't.

You stood next to me when others couldn't.

You are my love, my life, my wife.

I love you.

Bob

Acknowledgments

I would like to give special thanks to the following people.....

To my family, especially my mom, for always having faith in me and challenging me to always do my best in life.

To all of the residents of the great City of Westland for allowing me the honor of serving as their Mayor for so many years.

To Richard Dittmar for accepting the task of my campaign manager for three consecutive elections and for being my good friend.

To my administrative staff at the City of Westland for all their help. Thank you for always being there for me.

To Keith Madden for his advice and assistance with filing all the necessary legal documents along with your advice, in general.

To Tom Taylor, previous Mayor of Westland and author of the book, The Golf Murderers, for his advice and suggestions.

To Mike Reddy and George Riley, owners of the Fire Academy Brewery & Grill in Westland, Michigan, for always having a booth reserved for me to do my rewrites.

To Diane Fritz, the best clerk Westland ever had. Thanks for all your help reviewing the portions of the book regarding elections laws.

To Doug Gowen for his proofreading expertise and for placing a zillion red marks on my manuscript for me to correct.

To Barb Gunia of bj Graphics for the outstanding cover design.

To BookCrafters for making everything look so great.

To Joseph M. Marshall for his photo work on the back cover.

TABLE OF CONTENTS

About the Author

Robert J. Thomas was born in the City of Detroit on September 2, 1950, to a wonderful set of parents, John and Blanche Thomas. His family first moved to the City of Westland when Robert was about six years old. He began working for the City of Westland in September of 1970 as a water meter reader at the Department of Public Service, and for the next twenty years, he held many different jobs for the City including the position of dog warden, small bus driver, as well as many others. He swept city streets, plowed snow, graded gravel roads, trimmed trees, repaired water main breaks and even installed underground sewers for the City. During his twenty years of employment with the City, he was quite involved in the Union holding many various positions including the office of President for the Union, AFSCME Local 1602. He actually resigned from the Presidency of the Union to run for the office of Mayor in 1989.

Robert first began thinking about running for office in the early eighties. He carefully watched the political scenery and waited for what he felt was the perfect time to run and then in June of 1986 he made his decision to run in the 1989 election for Mayor. Over the next three years, he painstakingly and methodically put together a campaign plan that no one believed could be won. Everyone felt that since he was just a DPW worker with no political background, no money and no real support except a few friends and family, that he was wasting his time, especially when he was challenging one of the strongest political machines in the City's history. Of course, the mistake everyone made was underestimating him. That is exactly what he was counting on.

His strategy worked perfectly and he accomplished one of the greatest political upsets in Westland's political history. The primary was a four-way race. He beat out a former Mayor, who at the time was an

1

incumbent councilman, as well as another current councilman, to be able to face the incumbent Mayor in the November general election. They continued to underestimate him and he went on to win the general election by a mere two hundred votes. While two hundred votes is a very small margin of victory, it was simply amazing that he won at all considering the odds he was facing including the fact that he was outspent five to one during the campaign.

Robert was sworn into office and took the Mayor's seat on January 1, 1990. In November of 1993, he was again challenged by the same former mayor and current councilman who ran against him in 1989, as well as several other candidates. Once again, he proved that he could put together another winning strategy by making history on two fronts. First, he won the election by the largest margin of votes in the City's history of mayoral elections—over two to one, and secondly, he was the first Mayor in Westland's history to ever be elected to two consecutive terms of four years each.

In November of 1997, in his third Mayoral election and second reelection, he was challenged by a former councilman and another unknown candidate. Again, Robert proved his political prowess by winning with another landslide by getting almost sixty-two percent of the vote. He has never lost an election!

The continuing question among the so-called political experts was, "how does he keep doing this?" Robert has never shared any of his strategies with anyone but his inner circle and a few friends and family until now. In this book, which is designed with the first-time runner in mind, he will explain step-by-step how to put together your first campaign for local office.

About the Book

After serving over eight years and winning three consecutive elections as the Mayor of Westland, Michigan, known as **"the place to be,"** I felt compelled to share some of my experiences with those who wish to enter the political arena and serve their community on the local government level. When I first decided to run for the office of Mayor, I headed down to the local library to find some research material on how to run for local office. I was surprised to find out that there was no material to check out on the topic. My next stop was the local bookstores. I fully expected to find stacks of "how to" books on the subject of running for local office, but I was totally surprised to find that the material was scarce or non-existent.

This was quite frustrating. It was hard for me to fathom that with all the thousands of people who run for local office in all the communities across the nation each year, I could not find a simple, easy-to-read handbook or common-sense manual to help the average person run for local office. This book will change that forever!

As you can see, this book is not a novel. Sure, I could have written three hundred pages with lots of extra dialogue and graphs; however, it would take you three days to read it. That was not my goal. I wanted to keep it as simple and as condensed as I could and still give you the information you need. I believe I have succeeded. This book is an easy-to-read manual that is written in simple terms to explain to you, step-by-step, how to run for local office. Notice I said **local office** not state, or federal office. Although much of the information you will find in this book can be used in running for other levels of office, this book is specifically targeted toward running for the office of Mayor, Council, Township Supervisor or Trustee, School Board, County Commissioner, Township or City Clerk or Treasurer, or any other type of local office.

Also, as I give examples throughout this book, I may mention Mayor or City Council as examples more often than Township Trustee or School Board. I am sure that you do not want to read the titles of every possible office for every example I give. That would be a waste of your time. Just know that when examples are given, they apply to every type of local office available. And, while this book is designed for the **first-time** runner, if you are an incumbent or have run for any office before, I am sure that you will find this book full of useful information.

This manual will explain to you in detail and take you step-by-step through the process of putting together a campaign for local office including some of the problems you will face along the way and how to handle them. Along the way, I will tell you some true examples of real-life experiences in the political arena, some of which may be comical, and some that may make you wonder why anyone would ever want a life in politics!

I will not pull any punches in this book, since that would be a great disservice to you. I believe you need to know exactly what you are getting into because most people who enter the political arena have no idea. Politics is a tough game and is not for the meek or timid. Yes, I said "game," and that's exactly what it is, make no mistake about it. A tough game that is not played by any approved set of rules. Listen to this phrase and remember it well, *"all is fair in love, war, **and politics.**"* If you think for one minute that you are going to enter the game of politics and that all the players are going to play fair and adhere to some set of rules that treat all of the candidates equally, forget it, it will not happen! I wish it would and believe me there are many others in politics who wish that's the way it was, but it just **isn't!** The cold, hard reality is this: If you are going to run for local office you had better be prepared to face some very rewarding and unrewarding experiences.

Some of the things I will tell you are not designed to scare you away from your dream of being elected to local office, but if it does, I may have done you a favor and spared you from what could have been a nightmarish ordeal for you. I know of people who have run and won, only to cry out that they wished someone would have told them what they were getting themselves into. They left office when their terms expired never wanting another taste of politics again. Of course, you are one big step ahead of them since you have this book, which will explain to you what you are getting yourself into and what you will face in a campaign.

This book is written in a non-partisan fashion. I realize that many of you will be involved in running in partisan races, running as a democrat or a republican, or some form of independent party. However, many of you will be running in non-partisan races. For those of you who are involved in party races, you will need to follow the rules of the party you're involved with, and I can assure you that they will let you know what they are. You will not have as much freedom to campaign exactly as you want to if you are in a partisan race, but if that is the way your community set up its system of elections, you have to live with that. I am not going to refer to party throughout this book, but keep in mind that when we are talking about databases, raising campaign funds, and targeting certain voters, you will need to target your party, also. In other words, if you are a democrat, you need to find out who the democratic voters are in your community. If you are a republican, likewise. The voting records for your community should tell you who they are. Regardless of party, you will still need to concentrate on *"good voters,"* which is a term you will learn about later on in this book. Just keep in mind that the advice and strategy that is given in this book still apply in the same way regardless of whether you are running in a partisan or non-partisan race.

Let's talk about incumbent office holders versus newcomers. If you are the incumbent, you have an advantage. **Use it!** Don't listen to those who advise you not to take advantage of the fact that you are the incumbent. You have many opportunities that are not available to a new challenger and you should make use of them. Hey, you were the challenger before and you can be sure that the incumbent you ran against had those opportunities available to him or her. You can be sure that he or she used them! Again, while this book is designed for the first time runner, any incumbent will find this book full of ideas and strategies that will help you retain your office.

Now, to the challenger or non-incumbent. This book will give you the same knowledge, and probably more, about how to run and win elections for local office, than the incumbent that you are challenging. I have run in three consecutive elections for Mayor and I have never lost an election! With this book, you will have an advantage that most newcomers don't have. You will have the advice and knowledge that I have learned during three successful campaigns at your fingertips.

As you go through this book and listen to all the strategy and advice, please don't think for a minute that there are not many other ways to campaign and win an election. I am the last person in the world who will tell you that I know everything about politics and elections, because no one does. There are too many variables in politics and just as many opinions. There are thousands of ways to run and win a campaign. This book is a guide and it will give you the information and strategy to put on a very effective and efficient campaign. I have broken it down into the simplest and easiest terms that I could. This book will give you an advantage over all the other candidates in the race, and most likely, even the incumbent. You may come up with many ideas of your own during the process and don't think that just because you haven't seen it in this book, that it won't work. If you think it's a good idea, try it. If it's successful, write me a letter and I'll include it in the next edition of this book, and yes, I'll mention your name!

So, sit back, relax and take the time to read this manual from cover to cover. It will explain exactly what you will need to know and do if you decide to run for local office. It will serve as your guide as you go through the election process and you will even find yourself returning to this book over and over again. You may even want to order a few extra books to give to your inner circle so that they can study it between meetings. If you haven't started your campaign yet, do yourself a favor and read the entire manual before you get started. There are many pieces of information that will be useful to you in your early planning stages.

Chapter One

Getting Started

Okay, you have bought the book. That means you are either thinking about running for local office or have already decided to do so. In either case, you still need to re-think your decision one more time. First and foremost, this needs to be **your** decision. After all, you are going to be the candidate. However, it's a good idea to bounce the idea off family and friends. When I made my decision to run for Mayor, I got my family together at dinner and informed them of my decision. Some of them thought I was crazy and some thought I should give it my best shot. It helps to get different opinions, but in the end it must be **your** decision, not someone else's. That way, you won't have any regrets, or laying the blame on others later on.

After informing my family, I bounced the idea off a few close friends. I recommend you do the same. Make sure these are people you can trust to keep quiet, especially if you don't want this to be common knowledge just yet. You will be surprised how fast the news about a new candidate for Mayor or Council in a community can spread. Your friends can give you their thoughts on where you could get support for your candidacy and you can start asking them for their support if you finally decide to run.

One of the most important questions that you need to ask yourself is why do you really want to run? Are you mad about one particular issue in your community and you've decided to run for office so that you can affect that one issue? If that's the case, give this decision some more thought. Being an elected official is much more than taking care of one issue. There will be dozens of issues. What if you take care of the one issue that made you run? Will you be willing to tackle the many other issues that will certainly follow? I've seen people run on one-issue campaigns and end up being bored, resigning from office midstream, or even worse, losing their next election because they were ineffective in their first term.

Your decision to run should be because you really want to serve in the capacity of the office you seek. If, for example, you are going to run for Mayor or City Council, it should be because you want to help lead your community in the most effective manner and to tackle every problem that comes up and to be a part of the solution.

Also, don't run because you don't like the other candidates. I know of a person who ran for Mayor because he didn't like the other guy that was running. He won the election and really didn't want to be there or to take on the responsibility of the office. He turned out to be a poor leader for the community. Bottom line, make sure you're running for the right reasons, and be fully prepared to take on the responsibility of the office you seek. If you're running for the money you will make, don't. It certainly is not worth that. The truth is that most public officials are underpaid for the amount of responsibility they undertake and the tremendous amount of hours they have to put in. And, while there are truly some unforgettable and grand moments along the way, there are just as many unhappy events that can occur that can test the limits of your sanity.

You might be wondering then, why do people seek public office? The answer is quite simple, because they love the work and the challenge it gives them. One of the things I like best about my job as Mayor is that I have been able to gain a tremendous amount of experience that can't be bought at any price. I have been able to experience things that most people only dream of, and the knowledge that I have gained will help me through the rest of my life and in every decision I will make in the future.

If, after all that, your decision is to run, you need to do some research. That is the dilemma I faced in 1986 when I first decided to run for Mayor. I set out on a quest to find the basic information that I required to run for public office. I still wanted to keep my decision to run for Mayor quiet and I needed to do my research secretly, so I headed down to the local library in search of any books or publications available that would explain the process of running for local office. I was quite surprised to find almost nothing that would help me. Well, not being one to give up easily, I went to some other libraries and when that didn't pan out, I headed down to the bookstores. I could not find one publication, book or manual that explained the process of running for local office. This was quite a shock to me. I could find a book about anything else I wanted, from how to plant flowers in the spring to how to fix a television, but I could not find one book that explained in detail how to run for local public office. You won't have that problem since you now have this book.

When I first ran for Mayor in 1989, I made my decision to do so in June of 1986, a full three years prior to the actual election. I started to go to all of the council meetings, budget sessions and special study sessions going on in my community. I would suggest that you do the same. I was able to learn who all the players were and found out what was going on in my community. The Council and the Mayor wondered what I was doing there, but I kept quiet and just took notes and silently watched the process. More importantly, I watched how citizens reacted to the different issues that were going on, since I knew that I would have to put together a game plan for the election and I would have to hit the issues that were important to the majority of the community.

This is extremely important! Don't make the mistake of just automatically thinking that the issues that are important to you are important to the majority of the voters. Do yourself a favor and read that sentence again! If you want to win, you'd better be talking about what's important to the majority of the voters and not the minority. Make a list of the major issues that are important to the majority of the voters and base your campaign plan around them. Sure, you can throw in a few of your own special interests, but if they don't matter to the voters, don't make those the main focus of your campaign. If you do, you will surely lose the election. Remember, you want to win!

If, after considering all of this, and talking with your family and friends, you have decided to follow through with your decision to run, then the next chapter is very important. It may yet change your mind!

Chapter Two

Things You Need to Consider

This chapter may yet change your mind about running for office. Please understand that I am not trying to change your mind; I hope your decision ultimately will be to run. I simply believe it is my obligation to let you know that there are some really tough things that you will face if you do run. There are some cold, hard truths that you need to consider that you may not have thought of before or maybe just didn't know about. What I am about to tell you may scare you away from running for office, and if it does, then I have probably done you a huge favor. Not because I don't think you could handle the job of holding public office in your community, but if the cold, hard reality of politics scares you, I may have saved you from a nightmarish ordeal and from wondering *"why didn't someone tell me."* Well, this book's job is to tell you so you understand what you are getting into.

Running for office is much more demanding than you think and holding office is even more demanding. The campaign will consume almost all of your time. If you work a full-time job, you are already suffering a handicap. You will only have a few hours each weekday and believe me, the weekends alone are not enough. You will have to campaign three or four weekdays and most of the weekend.

Please face *this* fact. During the campaign, your family will come second. You will miss most dinners with the family and you won't be going to the movies much. Sure, you can schedule some personal time for you and your family, but if you think it will be like anything close to your current lifestyle, forget it!

Of course, if you're laid off or unemployed, you have a distinct advantage since you will be able to work full-time on your campaign and still have some time for your family. When I ran for mayor, I was a full-time employee of the community in which I ran. It was extremely difficult for me to run a full-blown campaign and work full-time. It's not easy, but it can be done. This is where you count on your family. They will have to cut the grass, paint the house or perform other normal tasks that you usually perform. Also, forget about your favorite hobbies; you will not have time for them. If you think you'll have time to go camping or boating or whatever your hobby is, forget about running and go to the campground. When the election is over, you can read the local paper while sitting in your lawn chair by the campfire and read about who won. You can be sure that the winner wasn't at the campground while you were there!

You will have to ask people for money! It takes money to run a campaign and unless you have a nest egg that you can dip into, you will have to raise money to finance your campaign. You, as the candidate, will have to be able to approach family, friends and even strangers to give you money. I will talk later about how to raise the funds you need. If you cannot do this, if you believe that you cannot ask people for money to fund your campaign, put this book down, go to a movie, and forget about a career in politics!

You will need to prepare yourself and your family for some pretty shabby treatment. You may be the nicest person in the whole world and you always treat everyone with respect and friendship, but you need to prepare to be surprised by how badly some people will treat you once you run for political office. It may be wrong and unfair, but it is one of the cold, hard realities of politics and you just have to accept it.

There are people who are complete strangers to you that will publicly say terrible things about you even though you have never done or said anything to them. They will also come to events where you are either speaking or just attending and try to do political damage to you in any way they can. Some of them will make unfavorable comments about you to other people attending the event or simply spread some rumor about you that is just not true. Don't be alarmed. For some of these people, it is simply their assignment.

Many of these people are supporters of the candidate or candidates you are running against. They could just be friends of your opponent's supporters. Keep in mind, it really has nothing to do with you. It's just that when you enter a political race, you immediately make political enemies. I have always said that if God ran for political office in any community, at least one-quarter of the community would hate him the day after the election!

The most important thing to remember is this: If you cannot handle the shabby treatment and the stress that goes along with it, get out of the race, you don't belong there. If you think the treatment is bad during the race, it can get much worse after you win. Of course, if you lose, everyone will say what a courageous fighter and campaigner you were. I would much rather hear people say nasty things about me after I have won than to listen to them say nice things about me after I have lost the race.

The amount of money it takes to run a campaign can differ greatly. It will depend on the office you are running for, the population of the community you are running in, and the makeup of the community. It will depend on how many pieces of literature you put out, whether or not you mail them or hand deliver them, as well as how many yard signs you want to put out and whether or not you buy bumper stickers or other campaign materials. Of course, the more you have to spend, the better the odds you will have at winning. You will need to prioritize what to spend your resources on. In most elections, literature, yard signs and cable are the top priority, and all the other things such as bumper stickers, pins, hats, etc., are of a lesser priority. Every campaign is different, so you need to set your priorities based on your needs.

Ever heard the saying, *"you can't buy an election"?* That's not *entirely* true. Let me explain. You could have a candidate who is just terrible. Wrong message, lazy, hard to get along with and keeps screwing up everything. Or, you could have an incumbent who has done a terrible job and has never accomplished anything good for the community. No amount of money will help either of these candidates get elected or reelected unless they have no real opposition.

So, while I agree that you can't always buy an election, I have always believed that *"you can buy votes!"* If you have two candidates who are in a close race, and both candidates are doing an equal job and both seem to be projecting a good image and message to the voters, the candidate that has the most money will be able to get his or her message before the voters more often, and if you are that candidate, you will most likely be the winner. Now, this does not always hold true. Your message may not be the one the voters want to hear, so, even though you can get your message out more than your opponent's, it still will not help you. Remember what I told you in chapter one, **select the issues that are important to the voters!** This is vital to any successful campaign.

Since there are so many variables in any campaign, and in any community, it is impossible for me to estimate the costs of your campaign. However, I will try to give you some examples. If you are running for Council in a small community of around ten thousand people, you might spend anywhere from two to ten thousand dollars. My community, Westland, Michigan, is a city of eighty-five thousand. Most candidates running for Council will spend an average of six to ten thousand dollars on a campaign. Most candidates for Mayor will spend about twenty to thirty thousand if they are a challenger, and anywhere from thirty thousand to one hundred thousand dollars if they are an incumbent. The big disparity is because an incumbent Mayor can always raise a lot more money than a challenger. The lesson here is that if you are the challenger, you are going to have to substitute a lot of hard work and good old-fashioned elbow grease for money.

My first campaign was a good example of this. My opponent had approximately one hundred thousand dollars to spend on the campaign and he spent it. I, on the other hand, raised and spent about twenty thousand dollars on the entire campaign. He was the incumbent with a lot of political experience and a strong machinery behind him. I was a civil service worker with no political backing or experience. We had to make every dollar count as five. That's why we were so careful in targeting our voters and making the most of our postage dollars and printing. We had to deliver literature instead of mailing because we didn't have enough money and I made more visits to people's doorsteps than my opponent did. It worked. We won by a mere two hundred votes!

During the beginning of your campaign, you may be strapped for cash. It's common for new candidates to have to dip into personal finances to get started. It is important for you to find out about if and how you can **loan** your campaign money. I unfortunately found out about this too late. During my first campaign in 1989, I used about five thousand dollars of my own personal money to get started. I never realized that I could have listed this as a loan and paid myself back from future fund raisers. Don't make this mistake. This one bit of news alone may be worth more than a hundred times the cost of this book! Of course, in the state, county or community you live in, you may not have this opportunity, but you need to check to make sure, since in many instances, it is allowed.

While you may be surprised that I have given you more than a few reasons to decide not to run for office, there are so many rewards in store for you if you do decide to run. The rewards of the learning experience as well as the great feelings of satisfaction you will get from making your contributions to your community are just a few of many. In my personal opinion, the rewards outweigh the negative things that go with running for office. So, my advice, as long as you feel that you can handle the negatives that I warn you about in this book, is to *"go for it"!*

Chapter Three

Get Organized

Okay, now you've made the decision to go ahead and run. You've considered the good and the bad things I spoke about in the previous two chapters and you have decided to forge ahead. Great! You are on your way to a new chapter in your life that will be unlike anything you've ever experienced before. Now you have to get organized.

One of the first things that you need to do is find out what paperwork and forms need to be filled out for your political committee. Please keep in mind that every state, county, city, township or village may have different requirements and forms to fill out in order to run for public office. They can vary greatly, which is why you need to find out by doing some research first, to make sure you follow the rules correctly. If you have run for office in another state or community, don't just assume that everything is the same.

Your first stop should be at the local Clerk's office. You may find out that you have to go to the county or state elections division, but make that first stop at your local Clerk's. They should be able to give you the information you will need to get you started, and in many instances, you will be dealing with them for much of the process. One of the first things you will be picking up will be your nominating petitions. In some communities, you can pay a filing fee instead, but this rule can vary from community to community. Make sure that you check. Explain to them that you are interested in running for local office, and tell them what office you are seeking. They should be able to tell you where you need to start. If it's for Mayor or Council, or a similar office, you will be able to handle most of your business there. If you are running for a county office such as a county commissioner, you may be able to pick up the paperwork you need at your local Clerk's office, but you may need to file that paperwork at the County. Sometimes, the local Clerk's office will forward the paperwork to the County for you. If you are running for Mayor or Council, you will usually pull your petitions at the local Clerk's office. If you are running for a county office, you would normally pull your petitions at the county elections division. If you are running for school board, you may need to start at the board of education or the school district that you live in. However, many school elections are handled by city, township or county election divisions.

The rules for filling out and filing petitions also vary from community to community, but make sure you follow the procedure outlined to the letter of the law. There are rules as to who can circulate petitions on your behalf and rules as to how to fill out those petitions. There are specific deadlines, and in almost every case, the deadline is non-negotiable. In other words, if you are to file your petitions by four o'clock p.m. on a certain day, do not arrive at the Clerk's office at one minute after four to file them. By law, they should not accept them. If my opponent were to file late and the Clerk accepted them, I would challenge the legality of the petitions. Don't get shot out of the gate before you even get started, by filing late.

As a general rule of thumb, you will want to get ten to fifteen percent additional signatures over the requirement for a buffer. I would recommend that you yourself gather some of the petition signatures personally; the voters like that and it gives you a chance to start circulating within your community. Remember, people who sign your petition must be registered voters within your community. Here is what I did to make sure that I got enough qualified signatures. Before I started gathering signatures, I purchased the list of registered voters from the local Clerk's office and checked off the names on my petitions *before* I filed them with the Clerk. Also, I made sure I filed them early enough so that I could turn in extra signatures before the deadline and I always had extra signatures on hand just in case.

If you have people help you gather your signatures, make sure they understand the proper procedure as a circulator. If they do not follow the rules, your signatures will be invalidated. Each sheet of petitions stands on its own merit. In other words, if one sheet is ruled invalid because the circulator didn't follow the proper procedure, it does not affect any other sheet. Additionally, one invalid signature on a sheet does not invalidate the remaining signatures. However, if the circulator fails to sign and/or date the petition and follow the procedures outlined by local or state statute, the entire sheet of signatures will be invalid even if every signature is proper. The rules for circulating the petition are usually printed on the petition itself, but ask questions if you are not absolutely sure.

In some states, communities do not conduct a local, county, state or federal election. The election may be conducted at the county level. In these instances, you can usually pick up the necessary paperwork at the local Clerk's office, but you may have to file the paperwork at the county. Some local Clerks will forward the paperwork to the county for you as a courtesy.

In some cases, you have to file your paperwork at the State elections division. Again, always begin at your local Clerk's office whether it's a township, village or city. Make a list of questions before you go. Remember, the process and the rules may vary greatly from state to state, so it's your job to ask the questions. Plus, it may save you an extra trip back.

Let me give you an example of the paperwork you may need to file. In Wayne County, Michigan, where I reside, you must fill out what's called a *statement of organization* form. This form may have a different name in the community, county or state that you reside in, but the information should be similar. In most cases, you will pick up the forms at the county elections division, but many times you can get the forms at your local Clerk's office.

The general information that you will need to place on the form may differ from one community, county or state to another, but here are the basic types of information that you may be required to supply. You will need to create a name for your committee. Keep it simple. If your last name is Smith, call it the "Citizens for Smith" committee. It's easier for all those campaign contributors you will find later on to write on the checks. I have seen candidates come up with committee names that will not fit on any check I have ever seen! Remember, keep it simple.

You will also have to select a chairman, campaign manager and campaign treasurer on the form as well as the name and address of the bank where your contributions for your campaign will go. You can usually list yourself as all of the above if you have not selected anyone to fill these positions yet, except for the bank, of course, and you can always file an amendment form as many times as you like.

Go down to any local bank and inform them that you want to open an account and explain what it will be used for. The name on the account will be the name of your committee. The name of my campaign committee and bank account is *Citizens for Thomas*. For convenience, you may also want to ask for a credit card in the campaign committee name so that you can charge many of your expenses and pay the bill monthly. If you do not want to do that, you can always use a personal credit card, but you will have to keep a good record to designate which charges are personal and which are for the campaign. It would be better if you avoided using the personal credit card for any personal charges until the campaign is over. You can also reimburse yourself with a check from your campaign checkbook for campaign-related expenses, as long as you have a receipt to show for it. The charge card is a good way to keep records of all your expenses for the campaign. In most cases, the laws limit the amount of cash that you can spend at one time, so paying with a charge card or a check is the best way to handle your campaign funds.

Keep in mind that usually you will have to file campaign reports with the proper elections division about all of your expenditures and contributions before and after both the primary and general election, so having good records is critical. Keep in mind that some people will try to find anything they can to criticize you for. In my last reelection we had some people whose donations exceeded the contribution limits. It was an honest mistake due to a law change that we didn't find out about until after the contributions were given. One of the news organizations did a full-blown story on it, but when we corrected it and returned all the excess contributions, we never read a word about it in the paper.

While you are at the elections division, whether the county or local division, ask for any and all written information pertaining to your candidate committee. They will generally supply you with a booklet that has all the forms you will need. Ask for any other report forms, new updates, dates of when you need to file certain reports, campaign finance laws, etc. You need to make sure that you read all the material yourself so that you understand what you need to do and how to instruct your manager and treasurer to handle things. The laws that govern running for office change often and sometimes without notice. Don't get caught short, check for any changes or updates on a regular basis. Every time I call the County elections division, I always ask if there are any new updates that I should know about, and I do the same if I stop there for any reason.

Right now, you may be thinking that this is all too complicated, but rest assured, it is not. You just need to read all of the material, ask questions and then follow the rules. Most of this is very simple and you can always call on the local Clerk's office, county or state elections division. If you are really lucky, you will find someone who has already done all of these things before and will work on your campaign. Just make sure it's someone you can trust!

Here's a tip for you. When you make that first trip down to the local Clerk's office, try to make a contact in that office. Pick out one person and ask some questions pertaining to elections. Feel that person out and if you feel comfortable, make sure that you always deal with that person whenever you go there. If you can strike up a casual friendship with someone there, it will pay off many times over in the long run. A friend in the local Clerk's office can save you tons of wasted time, however, be careful. This can also backfire. While you will in most every case find hard working, honest people working in your local Clerk's office, you need to take into consideration that some of the Clerk's employees may be very good friends with the person that you are running against. In Westland, we have one of the finest Clerks in the State of Michigan. Her name is Diane Fritz, and every one of her employees have been trained to give every candidate the correct information and to treat them all with respect. Again, make sure that you feel comfortable with the person that you deal with.

While the reporting requirements may vary from state to state or community to community, you will generally be required to file a campaign financial report before and after every primary and general election. The reports will detail how you raised your money and how much, who donated the money to you, what you expended the money on (literature, signs, bumper stickers, etc.), and what is remaining in your account. Check up on the rules concerning "in kind" contributions where people donate materials or service, since in most cases, you need to report it. There are penalties for filing late, so make sure that you file on time. The penalties aren't the problem, it's the bad press you will get in the local media and trust me, ***they will find out!!!***

In some states, there are contribution limits that individuals can donate to a candidate. Some states have no limits. The limits can vary from what an individual can give to what a political action committee can give. Find out first what those limits are and make sure that your treasurer tracks the contributions. In almost every case, the contributions have to be in written form like a check or money order, not cash. I would recommend that you keep a computer file of all contributions and contributors. It will make it easier for you to file your campaign financial reports, plus you will be able to generate mailing labels from this file for future fund raisers. There are many off-the-shelf computer programs that will help you, including Microsoft Access and Excel.

This next topic is very, very, **very** important. You will need to pick your **"inner circle."** The size of your inner circle will depend on what office you are running for and the size of your community. There is no hard and fast rule on the numbers. In my case, my community has a population of eighty-five thousand people, and I usually keep six or seven people on my inner circle. These people should be people that you would trust your life to. They are the people who will know things about the campaign and about you that no one else should know, and these people should be the kind of people who know how to do something most people cannot do, _keep their mouth shut!_ You will be amazed at how your opponent and the news media can find out something about your campaign strategy almost immediately after a decision is made. Believe me when I say that most people cannot keep quiet. Once they know something, anything, the natural tendency is to tell someone that they "trust." Of course, then that person will tell someone that they "trust" and before the hour is up, your strategy is out and your opponent will preempt you.

Keep your inner circle down to the minimum you feel is necessary. Everyone will want to be on the inner circle, but you will have to deny some of those requests. Some of your personal friends will want to be on the inner circle; don't put them there unless you feel it is the best thing to do. Remember, you are not in this race to keep everyone happy, you are in it to win. If you want to hold public office you may as well start learning how to make the tough decisions now during the early stages of your campaign. Sometimes, family members will want to sit on your inner circle. I would recommend against it. I never had any of my family sit on my inner circle. Sometimes, your spouse or brother may get upset because you do not take their advice. They will feel that since they are "family," you should always listen to them. Try to select close friends or co-workers that you feel comfortable with. Everyone else, including your family, will have many other opportunities to help with the campaign by doing such things as putting up yard signs, answering phones, passing out literature, etc.

Your inner circle will be the heart of your campaign. They will plan the strategy, write the campaign plan, help write the budget for the campaign and set policy for the volunteer workers. They will be involved in everything that occurs and they will give you advice on all matters. When you select these people, select them also with the thought that you may want to appoint some of them to your staff or other positions if you are successful, but keep that to yourself during the campaign. Don't make any promises of appointments before the election is over. You will have plenty of time for that, but pay attention to the performance of your inner circle people and keep in mind that loyalty is extremely critical. The reason I suggest that you wait is that it is not uncommon to discover some facts right at the last minute of the campaign that may question the loyalty of some of your closest supporters. If you had already promised any of them positions, you are now going to have to change your decision and all of their friends and family will now hate you. You are going to gain enough enemies without any help from yourself, so don't put yourself in this position if you can avoid it.

When you and your inner circle begin to write out the campaign plan, here are some important things to remember. Pick your theme or what is more commonly known as your message for your campaign. Make out a list of the important issues that the community is concerned about. If you have been going to the public meetings and reading the local papers, you should already have a handle on this. For instance, maybe development of small retail shops is so rampant that the voters are upset. Maybe the desire to build a new library for the community is an issue. Crime, vandalism, gang problems, drug problems could all be important issues to your community. Your job, along with your inner circle, is to target the most important issues that concern the **majority** of the voters. Do some research, make some survey phone calls to residents and then formulate your campaign around those most important issues.

Once you have selected your message for the campaign, <u>stick</u> <u>with it!</u> I am sure that you have heard the saying, "don't switch horses in the middle of the stream," and it is so true in a campaign. Don't switch your message in the middle of your campaign. If you do, your message will get lost and the voters will become unsure of what you really stand for. You need to be committed to your plan from day one right up to election eve. This is why it is so critical to get the message right from the onset of the campaign. While we are on the subject of not switching horses in the middle of the stream, don't make one of the other mistakes new candidates make. After they win the primary election, they go out and change their hairstyle or decide to get those glasses they have needed but have been putting off. Don't change anything. If you are a woman candidate for office, don't change your hairstyle. Don't even change the length of your hair. It should stay exactly the same from the beginning of the campaign right up to the general election eve party.

Together, you and your inner circle will need to formulate a budget. Decide how much you will have to spend to run the campaign. Get some estimates on the cost of printing, yard signs, bumper stickers, advertising or whatever else you decide to use to get your message out to the voters. The budget will change during the course of the campaign, but it helps to have a guide early on so that you can set fund raising goals to meet your needs.

Once you have written out your campaign plan, protect it. Do not share the information with anyone who does not need to know, even family. For emphasis, let me repeat this rule. Do not share the campaign plan and strategy with anyone who does not need to know! I followed this rule so closely that when I met with my inner circle, I supplied each person with a copy of the plan and an agenda for the meeting, and when the meeting was over, I collected the copies from each member. It wasn't because I didn't trust my inner circle, but accidents can and will eventually happen. Maybe one of them might leave it laying around where someone could see it or maybe they might stop at a car wash leaving the material laying on the back seat of the car and the guy cleaning the inside of the car is a supporter of your opponent. This is not paranoia, these things really happen. It's just that your plan and strategy is critical to your success and you must keep it protected.

Chapter Four

Your Database

You need to create your database of what I will consistently refer to in this book as "good voters." You need to burn the term "good voter" into your brain. Setting up the database is the area where new candidates make the worst mistakes and waste the most money in their first campaign. Either they set it up wrong or they don't set it up at all. Yes, you can buy labels directly from the Clerk in most cases, but they will most likely not be willing to print you out the "customized" walking lists that you will need.

I have often heard new candidates proudly exclaim that they are going to personally stop at every house in town and ask for support. Well, that may be a noble thought and it may be the way it has been done in the past, but it does not win elections, today. If any of my opponents in the race made that statement, I would offer to buy the gas for their car! I would challenge them publicly in the news media to live up to their claim and I would make sure that the news media checked to make sure. Meanwhile, I would be visiting at least five times the number of good voters they could visit in the same night. After all, __I__ didn't make that claim and if my message is one the voters want to hear, who do you think has the better odds of winning? I learned early on in my first campaign how important my database was, and I made sure that I created it right the first time.

Let me explain what a "good voter" is. You will hear me refer to this term "good voter" often throughout this book. He or she is the voter who will most likely vote in the election that you are going to run in. Let's use my first race as an example. When I went over the records at the Clerk's office in 1988, I found that the population was about eighty-five thousand people. Out of those, about sixty thousand of them were registered. However, upon further checking, I found that only about forty-five thousand of them were considered as active voters, which meant that they voted at least once in a four-year period. The incredible thing that I discovered was that only about sixteen thousand of them actually voted in the previous Mayor's race in 1985. These are the people that I considered "good voters." These are the people who I sent literature out to. These are the people I visited at their doorstep to ask for their support.

In my latest reelection campaign in 1997, there were about fifty-six thousand registered voters out of a population of eighty-five thousand people. Of that, approximately eleven thousand, four hundred actually voted for Mayor in the general election in November of 1997. That's only about twenty percent. That means that approximately only two out of ten registered voters actually voted. Let's go a little further. In the primary election of August 1997, approximately six thousand people actually voted in the primary election for Mayor. That's about ten percent of the registered voters. What does that tell you? About one out of ten people voted in the primary. Approximately one house in seven actually held a person that voted in the primary. Now, would you go to every house when you can easily find out who and where the good voters are?

This is called <u>targeting the voter.</u> If you want the best odds at winning your election, you must target your voters. By using this method, you will save money, and at the same time, increase your odds of winning, especially if your opponent has not learned this method yet. Here is what you need to do. Again, start at your local Clerk's office. They will most likely have the records there that you need and you can buy them as a hard copy or in electronic form such as on a computer diskette. If you are running for Mayor, ask for the list of people who actually voted in the last Mayor's race. If you are running for City Council, ask for the list of people who actually voted in the last Council

26

race. The same applies no matter what office you are running for. Just make sure that you are asking for the general election results in those elections. The people who vote in the primary are important, but you can always break out the records of the primary election voters from the general election voters for later use.

In some communities, there are elections for City Council or Township trustee in off years when there is no Mayoral or Township Supervisor race. This usually happens when the Mayor or Township Supervisor have terms of four years. Even when Township trustee or Council terms are for fours years, there are usually elections for these positions every two years. If this is the case, and you're running for Council or Trustee in an off election year, then get the list of voters who voted in the last off election year as long as it's not more than four years old. If the list is six or eight years old, it may be too inaccurate to trust. If that happens, get the list I spoke of in the last paragraph.

You also need to ask for the voter history. You will want to know the elections that each of the good voters actually voted in. That way, you can separate the good voters that voted in the primary as well as the general election. Remember, many of the good voters will not vote in the primary race! If you end up with a list of ten thousand good voters from the Clerk's office, you can almost bet that only about six thousand of them will vote in the primary election, and the great news is that you can pinpoint exactly who they are! By asking for the voting history, you can see who voted in the last general election, but didn't vote in the primary. There are many people who for some reason or another have decided that they will let others decide who makes it through the primary, and then they will vote for the candidate of their choice in the general election. I agree this does not make sense, but it is true in almost every community. I will explain later how you can use this information to your advantage by saving time and money while increasing your odds at winning. Just make sure that you include this information in your database.

When getting your data, ask the Clerk's office for a list of precincts and how many people voted in the last election of the office you are running for. Also, ask for several copies of the precincts map for your community. If they don't have enough, order them or ask where you can get some more. Usually, they are available at the engineering or department of public works departments. You will need these maps to determine the location and boundaries of each precinct and you will need these maps for walking door to door as well as for your sign crews. Some communities may be divided into wards or districts. Get the number of registered voters in each precinct and compare it with the number of people who actually voted in each precinct and you will get a percentage of registered voters who voted in the last election in each separate precinct. You will find that this number will vary greatly. You may find precincts where as many as forty or fifty percent of registered voters actually voted, and you may find some precincts where as little as nine or ten percent of the registered voters actually voted. This information is important. When you begin your door to door walking and you need to maximize your time, you can select the precincts where the highest percentage of registered voters actually voted.

Also, do not include newly registered voters, since they have not voted in any election yet. The same percentages will apply. Only about ten percent will vote in the primary and twenty percent in the general, but the problem is, you will not know *who* they are until they vote in an election. Stick with the good voters.

At this point, you might be thinking that many of these people have moved or maybe passed away, etc., and the list will be very inaccurate. Not true. You will find that while you will have some of those, the percentage will be small. I was surprised myself when I went door to door walking, using my list. I had the names of the people who lived in the houses I stopped at and it was unusual for someone to say that that person did not live there anymore and that they were new residents. Yes, I had some, but I would say that my list was ninety-five percent accurate! Not bad for a four-year-old list. Of course, after I won the election, I immediately updated my list and used all the people who just voted in the election for Mayor that I ran in. The numbers did not change much. On the average, only about twenty percent of the registered voters will vote in any local general election, and it is even less for the primary. Just check the data at your Clerk's office. Ask the percentage of registered voters who voted in the last few elections. You will be surprised to see how small the number is.

There are other data companies where you can get voter information for your community or any city, township, village, county or state. These are national database companies and you can find some of them listed in various campaign magazines. This data can be very helpful and informative. However, I have always found the data at the local Clerk's office to be the most accurate.

The point here is, how smart is it to spend a lot of money and effort on people who are not going to vote, when you can find out who they are? If you were a door to door salesperson selling vacuum cleaners, wouldn't you be delighted to have a list of addresses where people were going to buy a vacuum cleaner in the next few months? All you would have to do is convince them that your product is the one to buy! Well, selling your candidacy to the voter is much the same. You have to convince the voter that you are the better choice, but isn't it great to know that practically every voter you are talking to will actually vote in the election that you are running in! Please do not take this advice lightly. If you stop at every house, and your opponent stops at only the houses that contain people who vote, and you both have the same amount of time invested, your opponent will most likely defeat you!

Here is another good reason to target your voter and skip the non-voters. For some reason, and I do not know the answer as to why, but in most cases, the non-voter will take up more of your time talking to you when you stop at their house. I know, I have tried it. They will complain about everything under the sun, but they still do not vote. There are differing theories on this, but the answer really doesn't matter. The fact remains that if you stop at the non-voter's house, you will probably spend four times as much time as you would at a good voter's house. Good voters are generally well informed about what has been going on in their community, and they read up on the issues and candidates, so you don't need to spend much time with them. In many cases, they will tell you within the first three minutes who they are going to vote for. If it is not you, thank them for listening and get moving to the next stop.

So, now that you have the list, how will you use it? Find an off-the-shelf program to utilize it such as Microsoft Access or Excel or any of a dozen other programs to manipulate the data. I have used Microsoft Access along with Microsoft Excel in the Microsoft Office package. You can transfer the records back and forth between the programs to print walking lists and labels quite easily. If you are unfamiliar with computers or these programs, find one of your volunteers who knows about computers and they will gladly donate some time to setting it up so that it works easily for you. Make sure it is someone you can trust. Remember, this person is going to know everything about your database. Do this early so that you are not waiting at the last minute trying to work out the bugs. Actually, I would recommend getting your database set up in the computer early enough to print out a few copies of your walking lists and a few sets of mailing labels before the campaign officially begins. In my first campaign for Mayor, I had all of my database set up in the computer at least six months before the official start of the campaign, which is the day the petitions are filed and cannot be pulled back. Doing this will save you time when you will need it the most. The worst thing that can happen is you are ready to begin walking door to door and there are no walking lists ready yet. Make sure that you do test runs on everything that you will print out from the database. Now that you have this very powerful tool, let's get into how you are going to actually use it to print walking lists, mailing labels, etc.

The most important thing you will do as a candidate, especially in your first run for office, since you will be an unknown candidate, is to go walking door to door introducing yourself and asking voters for their support in the election. For that, you will need walking lists with the names and addresses of all the good voters. Most communities will have the areas of the community divided into precincts. Some will be divided up into wards or districts, but for the purpose of giving examples, we will use precincts. My community is divided up into 40 precincts. You will want your walking lists printed out by precincts. Many communities will have a few precincts listed just for the purpose of filling in the absentee ballot vote. These are not real, physical precincts where people actually show up to vote so you will not create walking lists for those. Absentee ballots are either mailed or dropped off at the Clerk's office. In other words, I had a total of 40 walking lists that I used, one for each physical precinct. Let's say you're printing out precinct one. You want to print it out by street alpha, and the addresses going either up or down. Also, ask for a page break between each street, that way you can hand out one or more streets to an individual. For example, if one of the streets in precinct one is named Avondale, it will show up first and all the houses on Avondale will be listed first before the remaining streets. You will also want the computer to sort the addresses on Avondale in ascending or descending order. That way, your list for precinct one will look something like this:

Precinct	Address	Street	First Name	Last Name	Year
1	10101	Avondale	John	Doe	1943
1	10105	Avondale	Jane	Smith	1970
1	10110	Avondale	Tim	Jones	1957
1	10115	Avondale	John	Kramer	1975
1	10115	Avondale	Sue	Kramer	1960

This is just a sample and you can set your list up however you want, but here are some reasons I set mine up this way. As you can see, you can go up the side of the street that has the odd number addresses first and then come back down stopping at the even number addresses. The birth year in the last column is important information. The older a voter is, the more likely they are to vote and to be what is called an absentee voter, one who votes by mail. Absentee voters can make up as much as thirty percent of all votes cast in any election, and on the average they are fifty-five and older. Spend a little more effort and time with these "young" seniors, it will pay off later. You should be able to

31

have your database actually show who the absentee voters are by including a field for that. You can signify it with an "A" or a "P" or whatever you want. Notice on the list that there are two good voters in the house at 10115 Avondale. You get a double hit by stopping there. Some houses will have three, four, five or more "good voters." I will explain later how you can capitalize on that. Before you begin your walking in the neighborhoods, make up at least one complete set of walking lists for your entire community. You will also use your database to print your own labels for mailing letters and literature to the voters. You should have your system set up so that you can print out labels for just one street, one age group, absentee voters, one precinct, several streets, an entire subdivision or the entire community. This gives you the options you may need. Again, I would print at least one complete set of labels for the entire community ahead of time. I recommend that you make a list of the labels you feel you will need and print them all up ahead of schedule. Trust me, when the campaign gets heated up, you would be surprised how important and how difficult a simple task like printing a set of labels can be.

You can also set up your database to print out labels with Zip + 4, which can cut your mailing costs. You can even do bar coding. It will take more effort and additional volunteers to sort the pieces of mail to qualify for this and that is a decision you need to make. Talk with your local post office to get the information you will need. When you go to the post office, make sure that you talk to the person who works in the bulk mail area. There are several different ways that you can save on postage, but each one of them will cost you in time and work. Again, it's up to you to decide which trade-off is worth it to you. I have always used straight bulk mail. It is usually a thirty percent discount from first class mail and it is simple to use. The mail simply has to be sorted by zip codes, and in most communities, there is only one zip code. If you're going to run for office in a large city of over a hundred thousand population, you may want to consider the other alternatives to straight bulk mail. You'll be mailing enough to save quite a bit of money and you will probably have to do some sorting anyway.

Chapter Five

Walking Door to Door

This is, by far, the single most important thing that you, the candidate, will do in the election. If there were only one thing that you could do in the election, it would and should be walking door to door. History has proven time and time again that door to door campaigning is the most effective method of campaigning, and the best news is that it is the **cheapest** method! You **must** go out and stop at people's doorsteps and ask them to support you in the election, especially since most people probably do not know who you are or what you stand for. If you are the incumbent it is still important for you to do this, but it is not as critical as it is for new candidates. Incumbents have name recognition already and can sometimes win elections without going door knocking, although they will always increase their odds if they do! As a new candidate, however, you **must** do this! This chapter will go into detail as to how to do your door knocking so as to increase your odds of winning. If you have already set up your database like I explained earlier, you are already way ahead of your opponent. Remember, your list has only the "good voters" on it.

Before you actually start, you need to make an important decision. Whether to stop at every house on your walking lists or to maximize your time by just going to houses that meet specific criteria. This will depend on how much time and volunteers you will have and how large your community is. I would only consider doing this if you discover that you will not have enough time to visit at least sixty-five percent of the good voters before the primary election. Here is what I mean by meeting specific criteria. If you have set up your database as I

33

recommended, you will know which houses contain people who will vote in both the primary and the general election. You will also know which houses contain people who will vote only in the general election, but not in the primary. You could print two separate walking lists but I would recommend using one list for each precinct. You will want to place a field on your computer list that will signify which voters always vote in the primary. That way, if you needed to maximize your time, you could only stop at houses that contain people who always vote in the primary and eliminate stops at houses that contain people who will only vote in the general. These primary voters will probably make up about sixty-five percent of your total good voter list.

Another option besides only going to primary voter households is to only go to multiple voter households. You will notice on your list that there are households that contain two, three, four, and in some cases, five good voters or more. If you need to maximize your time, you can skip past the single voter households and only stop at multiple voter households. I can tell you from experience that this **really** works. If you are concerned that some people will get upset that you passed up their house, don't worry too much. I never ran into that problem and no one ever complained to me that I passed their house. Most of the time, they don't even notice, and the fact that you stopped at one of their neighbor's houses is still a plus because the neighbor will mention the fact that you were in the neighborhood.

Here is how to decide if you need to use any of the methods I just mentioned regarding multiple households or primary voters when walking. You should be able to tell from your database how many households are in your community. Use as an average the fact that you will spend about five minutes at each house. Calculate how many people will be walking in the campaign and how many hours all of them, including yourself, will walk during the campaign and then calculate how many houses you and your team can stop at during the primary and during the general. If you are in a small enough community, you may be able to do all the walking yourself and that is even better. If you are not going to be able to cover at least sixty-five percent of the good voter households before the primary, you probably will need to visit just primary voters and/or multiple voter households when walking. Personally, my first choice is the multiple voter over the primary voter. I believe that it is less confusing and easier. If you can cover at least sixty-five percent of them, I would recommend that you go to all the households on your list. If you are really stretched for time, you can use both criteria by selecting those homes that hold people who vote in the primary election and hold at least two voters per household. Remember, your lists contain only the "good voters." Also, you can adjust your method depending on how you are doing. If you have too many rain days or if other problems arise that cause you to lose ground, switch methods accordingly.

Speaking of rain days, I was out walking door to door during my first campaign and it began to rain. Just a light mist, not enough to get soaked. I decided to keep going, and to my surprise, I found it to be very productive and effective! First, only go if it's a light rain, just enough to probably keep your opponent off the streets and home watching cable. If the rain is too heavy, everything gets wet and the voters will wonder if you have enough sense to come in from the rain. If it's just raining lightly, they will think of you as a dedicated candidate who will forge ahead no matter what the obstacle. They will respect you for it and they will **remember** you for it, which is great for you. They will tell all their neighbors how you came to their door "even in the rain" to ask for their support. Also, you will make better time since most voters will be sympathetic to your plight and will not keep you at the door very long. Walking in a light rain is a great way to outpace your opponent. If you don't believe that this works, just try it once and you'll see. Again, make sure that it's a light rain.

You will want most of your inner circle to go door knocking also, so that you can cover more homes in one evening. You can usually set them up in teams and you can either send them in different areas of the community or you can all work the same neighborhood at once. Not every volunteer can go door knocking. It takes the right personality to talk politics with people and they will have to be trained and briefed

35

about your position on all the important issues. Explain to them just how important it is for them not to "guess" at what your position on any given issue is. This incorrect information could cost you a lot of support in the election. If they are not sure, they should tell the voter that they will have you or someone who knows the answer for sure call them if they would like. You can also team up with one of your inner circle when you go door knocking. Your partner can always tell the voters that he or she is talking to, that the candidate is right across the street and they will be able to see you. You get the same credit as if you were at their door. Let me explain what "credit" means. If the voter knows you are in the neighborhood or can actually see you down the street, they will give you credit for the fact that you actually took the time to walk their neighborhood asking for support. That tells them that you are serious and working hard to get elected. They figure that if you work hard at your election, you will work hard if you get elected. So, even though you are not at <u>their</u> door, they will give you credit for being out there, much more credit than if you just mail them a piece of literature.

Here is a good way to cover a lot of ground and get some extra credit with the voters. Take a group of six, eight or ten people out in a neighborhood door knocking. Make sure that all of them tell the voters they talk to that the candidate is just over on the next street, and if they would like to personally ask the candidate a question, that they will see that you stop by before you leave the neighborhood. You will not get that many people who will make that request, but you as the candidate will get almost the same credit as if you went to the door yourself. Meanwhile, you can bounce from street to street and door to door as the requests to speak to you come in. Here is another great tip. Don't go to the same area two nights in a row. Your opponent will be trying to track you and send in his or her workers to the same area you are working in, to try to negate your progress. If you work the same area more than one night in a row, he or she will surely find where you are. If you go to a different area each night or even every couple of hours, they may not get any reports about where you are. These are very effective methods of campaigning!

One thing to consider is when to start. There is a lot of debate about the starting date. Some say if you start too early, people will forget about you by election day. Some say that people do not even pay attention to elections or candidates until the election gets close. I have learned by experience that there is some truth to both theories. Keeping all of this in mind and knowing that you are going to need to visit as many people as you can, I would start door knocking about three months before the primary election. If, for some reason, there is not going to be a primary election, but only a general election, I would start at least four months before the general election. For the sake of example, we are going to assume that there will be both a primary and general election since that will probably be the case.

You are going to need to have an introductory piece of literature to hand to people once they answer the door. Go to the local print shop and have them print you some. Don't have them print it on paper stock, because you will be handling them all day and paper will not hold up. I recommend that you get your intro cards printed on sixty- or eighty-pound card stock, printed on both sides and about one-third the size of a normal 8½ x 11-inch piece of paper. This way, your introductory piece should fit in your pocket or a small compartment-sized clipboard. I would recommend the compartment-style clipboard over a regular clipboard since you can also store some of your material in the clipboard along with extra pens or pencils. You want your picture on the front of the card and then some basic information on the card. You need personal information like your age, where you grew up, who has endorsed you, where you work, organizations you belong to, etc. Just basic background, don't go into long details, you won't have room. Also, put down some of the big issues that you are promoting for your campaign. You will want to mention if you're married and how many children you have, if any, as well as any degrees you hold or certifications you have. Do not make the intro piece too wordy and use bold, big letters. Make sure that you also ask for their vote on election day by placing this in bold letters where it can't be missed! Some people will disagree with me on the next point, but I still recommend that you do not put down the election dates on your intro cards or any of your literature for the primary. The reason for this is that if you do, you cannot use it after the primary election, and the fact is that you can still use up much of that material in the general as long as you do not date it by putting the primary election date on it, especially your intro card and the sorry I missed you cards that I will speak of in a minute. The "good voters" that you have targeted will know when election day is.

You will have to put your disclaimer on this and usually on **all** pieces of campaign literature, so make sure your printer knows that. If your committee is called "Citizens for Smith," then at the bottom of the back of the card in very small letters print, *"Paid for by Citizens for Smith,"* followed by the address including the city, state and zip. Some states require that you list the treasurer, also; make sure you check. Also, make sure that you put your campaign phone number on the card. Most people just use their home line, but you can get an extra phone line installed if you wish and the cost can be charged to your campaign. Check with the elections division, but usually, you are required to put the disclaimer on **all** campaign material, except envelopes.

You will also need another piece when you go door knocking. It's called a "sorry I missed you card." It is usually referred to as a "door hanger," because it has an opening with a little slit in the top of the card so that you can place it over a doorknob. Make this card the same size as your intro piece so that you can actually keep some of both of them in your pocket or clipboard. Make them also out of card stock so that they will stay on the doorknob. Also, I recommend picking a color scheme and sticking with it. My colors were yellow stock with black ink. On the door hanger, you will only need to print on the one side. You want your picture on the top of the card. Just below your picture, the words "sorry I missed you," and just below that, your name. When you leave a "sorry I missed you card," make sure that you sign your first name somewhere around your picture to give it the personal touch. The only information you need after that is just some basic information, and a request for the voter to support you on election day. Your text can be whatever you want, but for example you could say, "I was in the neighborhood to talk to you about supporting me in my campaign for

(Mayor, Council, etc.). I hope to meet you next time and I hope I have your support on election day." Remember, do not date these door hanger cards. Keep it simple. With both the intro card and the door hanger card, you are prepared either way. If the voters are home, give them your intro card and talk with them. If they are not home, leave the door hanger there so they can see it when they get home. The quantity of cards you need will depend on the number of voters on your list. A good tip is to order extra. On the average, you will experience as much as fifty percent of the households with no one home.

Do not put any of these cards or any literature in the mailbox. It is against the law and you will have a problem if you do it. You might be able to get away with putting the cards *behind* the mailbox, but it is better to slip it between the doors or behind the address board or a dozen other places that are visible to the homeowner when they arrive home. Watch your volunteers for this problem because they will ultimately put some in the mailbox if you do not keep after them about it. The post office can charge you postage for any they find, but that is not the real problem. Someone will turn you in to the news media and you will read about how you "broke the law," and you can be sure that it will be on the front page of the local newspaper.

When you first start your door to door walking, you might run into several "no's" right off the bat. Maybe you will and maybe you won't. It really boils down to the luck of the draw. If this happens to you the first time you go out, **do not let this get you down!** Keep going and get the no's out of the way and find those positive responses because they are out there, trust me! Even the ones who say no the first time may change their mind before election day. So, please do not let a batch of "no's" discourage you. If you are going to get through this whole election process, you will have to be a lot tougher than that.

When you get to the first house on your walking list, you may be wondering what you will say. Don't feel unique or special because every candidate has faced this question. I faced this myself the very first time I went out walking. I practiced a dozen ways to open the

39

conversation before I got there, but when the door opened and there I was on a stranger's porch, I didn't quite know yet what I was going to say. Don't worry, it's not that hard and people are very understanding. Just be ready to say hi and hand them your intro piece immediately which usually gets them to open the door. As you hand them the piece, say something like this, "hi, my name is John Doe and I'm running for Council, Mayor, etc., in the upcoming election and I would like to ask you to consider supporting me. Here is a piece of literature that tells you a little bit about me and if you have any questions about me or what I stand for, I would be glad to try to answer them now if you like." You can vary the message any way you like, but keep the opening statement short. Most people will not question you but will take your literature and tell you that they will look at it and give you some consideration. Inform them that your phone number is on the card if they think of something later. Some will certainly ask you questions to find out more about you. This is where the tricky part comes in. You want to talk to the person long enough to get them to feel they know a little about you, but not too long, since you are on a schedule. I have had to talk to people for twenty minutes before I felt I could break off the conversation by apologizing for taking up so much of their time and that I had better get moving or I will never get to the next street. Usually that will do it.

Some people will invite you into the house or back on the patio for a cold drink and to sit down for a few minutes. **Try to avoid this as much as you can!** These people are usually just bored or have nothing to do at the time and just want to visit. You can go back and visit after the election if you want but you cannot afford to waste time during the election. They may even be a supporter of your opponent and they are just trying to stall you from getting too far down the street, and yes, that really happens. I've experienced it myself. Check for obvious signs like your opponent's bumper sticker on their car or maybe your opponent's sign leaning up in the garage. The best advice is to stay on the porch, get the job done as quick as you can and get on to the next voter.

You have to judge this yourself and use common sense. You have to be careful not to give the voter the feeling that you do not care about what they are saying or that you have no more time for them, but you also cannot spend too much time at each house or you will **never** make any progress. Remember, it's all in the numbers. Try to average yourself out to five minutes a stop. Here's how to do that. After your first night of walking, count how many houses you stopped at where you actually talked to someone. Then, take the amount of time you were out walking and divide it by the number of houses you stopped at and you will have your average. If it's over five minutes, watch yourself the next night and try to cut down the longer conversations. Once you get several nights under your belt, you will find that you should be able to get it down below five minutes per stop. You'll learn to pick out the ones who don't really want to talk much and those are the ones that you make your opening statement, hand them the intro card and move on. Always smile and be polite even if you run into a rude person! After all, maybe they had a rough day and later they may feel guilty about how they treated you and decide to vote for you to make up for it.

If you run into a house that is on your list and they have a yard sign up for your opponent, **do not pass that house up!** I have found through my own experience that this does not always mean that they have made up their mind. The sign may be there because a friend asked them to put it up, *not* because they are supporting your opponent. I know this sounds strange, but it really happens. I have to admit that when I first started campaigning, I passed up any houses on my list with my opponent's sign in the yard, but then one night out of curiosity, I stopped at one of them. What a surprise!

When the lady came to the door I started out by saying, "hi, I see that you have my opponent's sign in your yard but I at least wanted to stop by and say hi and give you some of my literature to look at just so you can compare the candidates." To my surprise, the woman informed me that they had not made up their mind yet who they were going to vote for and she called for her husband who was in the backyard and I spent about ten minutes talking with them. I discovered that they had put the sign in the yard at the request of a friend as a favor, not as a commitment to my opponent. By the time I left, they had asked me to put one of my

41

signs up in their yard and they removed my opponent's sign! After that incident, I made sure that I stopped at all the homes on my list, including the ones with my opponent's signs in the yard and I can tell you that I changed dozens of signs to mine before the election was over! Keep in mind that you will not change a large number of them over to you but it is well worth the effort. It is demoralizing to your opponent to see one of your signs replacing theirs and I believe that the residents gain respect for your tenacity to knock on their door even when they have your opponent's sign in their yard. The lesson here is to not let your opponent's sign scare you. Also, while you're talking to the voters, don't forget to ask for permission to place a sign in their yard. You will be surprised at how many people will let you. I usually wait until the end of the conversation so that I can get a feel for their level of support before I ask. If I feel that they are not supportive, I usually do not ask. If they seem somewhat supportive, I will end the conversation with something like "thanks for taking time to talk to me, if you have any questions later or would like a sign in your yard, you can call the number on the card and we will put one up right away." If they tell you to go ahead and put one up, tell them you have some in your car and you will stop and put it in before you leave the neighborhood. Make sure you do!

Once you are out campaigning door to door, you will eventually get the request to attend a "coffee hour" or a group of neighbors together in someone's basement or backyard. Sometimes, they will ask both candidates to attend. This is one of those tough decisions you will face, so let me give you some advice. If you can avoid attending these somehow, do so. Of course, it is true that you risk upsetting a group of people ranging from as little as four people to as many as twenty. However, in many cases, you can simply explain that your schedule will not permit it and try to send a representative or just some information or literature about you for their meeting. If you feel you have to attend any of these, request that at least 15 or twenty people show up for the event, which in most cases, that will not happen. The reason that I am recommending that you steer away from these types of events is simple, time.

Think about it this way. Even if the person can guarantee 20 people will attend the "coffee hour," you will probably spend at least two hours during this event. If it is in the evening of a work day, you can forget about any door to door walking. Now, out of the twenty who attend, how many of them will actually vote in the election? Remember, they are not being invited using your "good voter" list, so at best, about six of them. Out of those six, how many will you convince to vote for you? Again, at best, two-thirds of them, which is four. Now, compare that to how many "good voters" you could talk to if you had spent two hours out walking door to door. In two hours, averaging five minutes a stop and averaging just 1.5 voters in a household, you could talk to about 36 voters. If you could convince two-thirds of them to vote for you, that's 24 votes compared to 4 during a coffee hour! Remember, it's all about numbers. You need to reach as many "good voters" as you can before the election and you cannot afford to waste time talking to non-voters.

Now, that being said, you may feel a need to attend one of these functions. Maybe it's for a friend or maybe the event is being put on by someone in the community who is influential in the community and can affect a lot of voters with their support of your candidacy. Maybe you want to hone your skill of answering pop questions. It boils down to using judgment as to how important it is to winning the election. However, do not be afraid to say no and upset a few individuals. It is one of the tasks that come with being an elected official and you might as well get used to it.

Chapter Six

Campaign Literature

Probably the second most important piece of your campaign puzzle, with door to door walking being the first, is your campaign literature. This is another vital task for your inner circle. They, along with you, will decide what type of literature you will put out, whether or not it will be mailed, who will receive it and when, the quality of the literature, the amount of information and even the theme of the literature. Many of these decisions will be greatly influenced by the amount of money you have to spend on literature. If you are a newcomer, you probably will not have enough money to do what you would like. That can be a problem for you since literature, and especially postage, can be the most expensive part of your campaign. Also, you will need to **target** your literature, which means you will be sending your literature to only the "good voters" on your lists from your database.

You will need to go down to the post office and fill out the paperwork for a bulk mail permit. Try to deal with the same person in the bulk mail division each time and get to know that person. There is an application fee for the permit but it is well worth the money. The permit will allow you to save about 30% on postage for straight bulk mail. The more you mail, the more you will save. You cannot afford to mail out first class unless you live in such a small community that you will only be mailing out a few thousand pieces or less. Each time you mail with your permit, you will have to fill out a form that you will take to the post office with your mailing. You can get these forms ahead of time. Once you get your permit number, give your printer who will be doing your literature the number. That way, they can print your permit right on the literature so that you will not need to use an ink stamp or buy the bulk mail stamps. Any good printer will know how to do this as well as where the post office requires your mailing label to be. Here's a tip. Have your printer print your bulk mail permit on **all** your literature except your "sorry I missed you" card and your introductory piece. Even the pieces that you may decide to hand drop door to door. Why? If you are able to raise extra money, you may change your mind about dropping it door to door and decide to mail it and the permit will already be on the literature and ready to go. Otherwise, you will have to have the printer run it through the press again to put the permit on **if** you left the proper space for it, which is unlikely. Also, running a finished piece back through the printing process can damage some of the pieces and in some cases of folded literature, it usually cannot be done. And, in the end, if you do not mail it, the label area and permit doesn't take up much space and it doesn't cost anything extra to print it on the literature in the first place. So, be smart and always leave space for a label and print your permit on any piece of literature with the exception of your "sorry I missed you" cards and your introductory piece.

Your literature is very important since it is **your** story. It represents **who** you are and **what** you are. It says what **you** will do if **you** are elected. Make sure you take the time to decide what you want in your literature. Keep it simple looking and as brief as possible. Use large, bold letters. Do not write out long explanations of your position on issues with small text. **They will not read it!** Statistics have proven time and again that the average lifetime of most political literature is the time it takes to walk from the mailbox to the trash can. People will not read most of the literature. They will scan the headings and the big, bold letters, but most of the small print will go unread. When you are writing your literature, write out the first draft. Then take each paragraph and try to shorten it up while saying the same thing. Do this again and again until you have said what you want in your literature with the least amount of words for that piece of literature. If your literature is too wordy, trust me, most people will not read it. Select the most important issues to place in your literature. You cannot fit all the issues in your piece, so pick out the most important ones and make them stand out.

Make your literature simple and cost-effective. You can ask your printer to give you price estimates, but one very cost-effective way is to print your literature on a normal 8½ x 11-inch paper. Print it on both sides and fold it in half. You end up with four areas that are 5½ x 8½ inches. This is plenty of space and probably as much as anyone will read anyway. Use just 20# paper, white or color. Picking a colored paper and black ink is sometimes cheaper than using colored ink and can give you the same appeal. If you can afford two colors, such as black and red ink on white paper, it does set the literature off and you can use the color to get the voters to notice certain sentences or words. Don't overdo the color just because it's there. Remember, you want the color to make something stand out. Again, your printer can give you estimates on every different way you want.

How many different pieces of literature you get to put out and whether you can mail it or have to have it dropped door to door will depend on how much money you will have. There are ways to always maximize what you have and we will go into that later. Keeping in mind your resources, you should at least put out two pieces of literature to all the "good voters" in the primary as well as two in the general. Keep the same theme in every piece of literature even though you can adjust your discussion on the issues just enough so that it doesn't look exactly like the same piece you sent out the previous time. Let me give you an example. In my first campaign, two of the major issues I hit on were over development, and the lack of service. On the development issue, I might talk about the number of vacant strip stores in town in the first piece, and in the next piece I might talk about how we have been building too many apartment complexes and we should instead build single-family homes. Two different topics, but the same issue. On the lack of service issue, in one piece, I might talk about how we don't have the right equipment to provide the level of service we need, and in the next piece, I might talk about not having enough manpower, but again, the issue is the same. So, keep the same theme going throughout your literature. That way, the voters will finally lock on to what you stand for, and if they like your message, your odds of winning will increase dramatically.

I am going to assume that you will have enough money to do what I suggested was the minimum amount of literature for your campaign. With that assumption you will want to mail your first piece of literature about four weeks before primary election day. Your second piece should be mailed out at least one week before primary election day. Make sure you check on the timing of the post office regarding bulk mail. Usually, when it comes to political bulk mail, the post office will deliver it within two or three days from the time you drop it off, and sometimes, the very next day. Check with the bulk mail division of the post office to make sure. If they tell you it will take longer, adjust your schedule of mailing accordingly. Remember, a piece that gets there after election day, is quite ineffective.

If you do not have enough money, you have a few options. One, you can always use volunteers to hand drop your piece of literature instead of mailing it. This will save you money in postage, but it is not as effective as mailing, since many of your pieces will end up behind the bushes or blown down the street from the wind. If you hand deliver, you will have to explain to your volunteers how critical it is to make sure they affix the literature properly so that it does not fall off at the slightest breeze. The most common mistake is your volunteers will roll the literature up and stick it inside the handle on the screen door. Instruct your volunteers not to do this or you will find that much of your literature will just blow down the street. Make sure they place it somewhere so that it will not blow away. They can open the screen door and drop it between the main door and the screen, but only do that if the main door is closed. Also, if it rains before the people pick it off the door, most of it will be ruined. Now, to really save money by hand delivering, you will need your volunteers to only drop at the houses that hold the "good voters." This will cause a lot of extra work for the volunteers. They will have to carry the list and go by it. The other option is to print more pieces of literature and have them drop a piece at every door. This will increase your printing cost, and while it will still save you money in postage, the savings are much greater if you only print enough for your volunteers to drop one piece at the doors of only the "good voters."

47

Another way to save money, and I recommend this way over the previous way of hand dropping, is to mail only to the people who vote in the primary election. This can cut your postage costs by almost half. Even if you have enough money to mail two pieces of literature to all the "good voters" in the primary, you may want to mail three pieces to all the primary "good voters," or two pieces to the primary "good voters" and one to all the "good voters," instead. You will save money in postage and get more bang for your buck. I have done this repeatedly and it works! You can also maximize your postage even more by mailing to all the "good voter" households that hold at least two or more voters. This can cut your postage dramatically, and postage is one of your biggest costs in a campaign. You can save even more postage cost by instructing your volunteers to only mail one piece of literature to each house on your good voter list. If there are multiple voters in a household, place each label over the other, leaving only the name showing on all the labels above the last label. The last label will have the address on it. Trust me, this does not bother people who receive the literature in the mail this way. Actually, I've heard comments about how candidates *waste* money by mailing three or four of the same pieces of literature to the same house.

Pay close attention to this next tip. This is one of the easiest ways to save money in any campaign and at the same time increase the effectiveness of your campaign literature. Don't use envelopes for your short pieces of literature or letters you send out in the campaign. Many pieces of literature are simply letters sent out to voters asking for support. Some pieces of literature are just a letter-size piece of paper, printed on both sides, with up to four colors and tri-folded. Most people will stuff the literature in an envelope. This is a waste of money. Don't do it. You can save both time and money and increase your literature's effectiveness by simply sending the piece in the mail without an envelope. Let me explain.

First, envelopes cost money. Sometimes, more money than the literature stuffed inside it. Secondly, it takes volunteers hours and hours to stuff the literature or letter into the envelope and you have to schedule the envelope stuffing event and find some place to do it. Third, most campaign literature has a short life expectancy, usually the time it takes the person to travel from the mailbox to the garbage can. If your literature is stuffed in an envelope, the person may not take the time to open the envelope and never sees it. If you simply send it folded, with your picture, name, and a request for support on one side, at least the voter will see your name and photo before it hits the garbage can. And, the odds are now in your favor that the voter will open the literature and take a peek at the rest of it. Success! You have now saved money, time, and increased the effectiveness of your literature. Think about this. The last time you received a piece of political literature, was it in an envelope? If it was, did you care one way or another. Probably not, so why waste the money and why make the voter take the time to open the envelope just to see your literature? Plus, you can take credit for saving some trees by not using envelopes which just get thrown out. I can tell you that during my first campaign, we spent thousands of dollars on envelopes. In my last reelection campaign in 1997, we used zero envelopes for literature and saved lots of money and time. And, my volunteers were delighted that they didn't have to stuff literature. They simply had to put the label on one side and count the pieces. They thanked me many times over and they got the work done in one-third of the time. Don't waste time and money on envelopes!

As you can see, there are many ways to save money and to maximize your resources if they are limited. The tips in this chapter alone will save you at least ten times or maybe even one hundred times the cost of this book! You need to discuss all of these with your inner circle and decide which ones are right for you. Maybe you will come up with other great ideas, and if you do, drop me a line and let me know so I can pass it on to others. If I'm able to use your tip or idea, I will make sure that I mention your name and where you're from.

Here is another very effective tactic to use that your opponent will probably never think of. I used this tactic in my first reelection campaign. I wanted to do something totally different that the voters would notice. As you look at your database, you can see where there are three or more "good voters" in one household. Your database will even tell you their first names, which is what you want. I sat down in the evening while watching television and hand wrote letters to every household that held at least three "good voters." I started each letter addressed to all of the first names. Say, for instance, you come across a house with four voters in it and their names are Sandy, George, Bob and Greta, I started out the letter with, Dear Sandy, George, Bob and Greta. I then hand wrote the letter. Each letter, to each family, was a different handwritten letter! I even addressed the envelopes by hand, personally! That way, if anyone accused me of printing them or having other people write them, I could prove that it was my handwriting. I used red ink, so that it would stand out and the people could see that it was not print, but actually ink. My close supporters thought it was too much work, but I disagreed. The family that receives this handwritten letter will know that you personalized it to them and they will make sure that each family member it is addressed to gets to read it. It worked great and I had people mention these letters for years after the election. It was unique and different which is what you need to do to stand out from the rest. You may want to only use this tactic in the general election so as not to give the idea to your opponent, but it would work just as well in the primary. You and your inner circle need to make that decision.

Also, you should do one separate mailing just to what is commonly called the "permanent absentee" voters in both the primary and the general election. This is very important to do. Your database should be set up so that you can sort out the absentee voters as a group and print mailing labels for them. You should address it to them as a group. I usually send them a letter instead of a piece of literature and it starts out, "Dear Absentee Voter." Remember, don't use envelopes. You can have your printer tri-fold the letter and put your permit and a spot for the mailing label on the outside back of the letter. It looks more personal that way and it goes over well with the absentee voter. They do not have to open an envelope, which can be difficult for some elderly people, and, as I said on the previous page, you save the cost of envelopes, which can be very expensive. Don't staple them either. Since the majority of absentee voters are seniors, you will want to mention your support for senior-related issues, but don't leave out your major issues that are in your other literature. Not **all** absentee voters are seniors. Timing is extremely critical here. The ballots for absentee voters do not go out on any exact day; it can vary for a lot of reasons. There are many candidates who end up missing the target and their literature gets there **after** the absentee voters have already received their ballots and voted. This just happened in the last election I was involved in to one of the candidates. He missed it by just a few days. This is where it pays off to have a contact person in the Clerk's office who will tell you exactly when the ballots are going out. If you can't be sure that you have the correct date, **mail them early!**

Another piece of literature you should create is usually called a support postcard. You can have these printed up early in the campaign so that you can distribute them to your friends and supporters in both the primary and general election. These are small postcard-sized pieces of literature, printed on a card stock. There are many ways you can design these postcards, but most of them are designed like this. On one side of the card, your picture would be on the left side. Just under your picture would be your name and the position you are seeking. Just to the right of your photo, there should be a short phrase, in bold text that would say— **"I'm supporting** (name) **for** (office) **and I hope you will, too!"** This text should be at the top of the right hand side of the postcard, leaving the bottom half blank. I'll explain why in a minute. On the reverse side of the postcard, you should put down some information about you and your candidacy. There won't be much room, so choose your topics carefully and prioritize what you want to say. Leave a spot for the postage and a spot for the mailing address. You can have your printer print your bulk mail permit on these postcards, but I recommend that you use a regular, first class postage stamp on these cards if you can afford it. Here is how you use these postcards.

You generally don't mail these postcards out yourself. You hand these cards out to your friends, campaign workers and supporters. When you have rallies or gatherings of your supporters to label literature, have them available for your supporters. Make sure that you have already put the first class postage stamp on these cards. Ask your supporters to take several of these cards and mail them out to their family and friends. Remember when I told you to leave a blank space on the bottom right of the front side of the card? Here's why. Ask your supporters to write a short personal note to their friends and family and personally sign it. Then, on the back where you have left space for the address, have your supporters hand address the cards to whoever they are sending them to. This adds a personal touch to this postcard. When people receive these cards, they are hand signed by someone they know, and they are much more likely to read it and give you more consideration. The amount of cards that you will use will vary depending on the size of your community, but you will not use that many. The average supporter will mail out a dozen or so to friends and family. I only printed and used a few thousand of these cards for both the primary and general elections and my community has a population of eighty-five thousand. Another option is to have your supporters fill out the cards and return them to you or the campaign manager, and then take them to the post office.

Assuming that you make it victoriously through the primary election, and that is what we are going to assume, you are in for some extra help and your resources will grow dramatically. You are now a viable candidate and it will be easier for you to raise the money you will need for everything, including your literature. Again, you will need to put out at least two pieces of literature, and hopefully three, in the general election, to all the "good voters," as well as one letter to the absentee voters. Unlike the primary, where you can mail to just the primary voters, when you mail literature in the general election, you have to mail to all the "good voters" on your list, with a few exceptions that I will mention in the next paragraph. This will cost you more in postage, but again, you should be able to raise more money now. Of course, there are still ways to save some money.

One way is to not mail your first piece in the general election to the absentee voters, since you will be sending them a letter addressed especially to them. You can also use this trick in the primary. Another way is to substitute your first mailing with a mailing to just multiple households that hold at least two voters. Your last piece of literature in the general should at all costs go to all the "good voters." That is not the time to skimp unless you have no choice. You may discover other ways to maximize your money and resources. You can adjust your methods and strategy as you go along, but the bottom line is, that you **must** get your message out to the voter one way or another. You do not have a choice if you want to win.

Each time you and your inner circle sit down to write another piece of campaign literature after the campaign is underway, you will ultimately face the decision of whether or not to answer the claims your opponent is making in his or her literature. Your first inclination will be to answer every claim. That is a common reaction, and every candidate feels the same way. The smart candidate will refrain from doing this. If your opponent discovers that you will use your valuable literature resources to answer what he or she is printing in their literature, they will lead you and your team around by the nose by continually bringing up issues in their literature that will keep you busy and off track answering them. Don't fall for that. If you do, the voters will never hear your message clearly, because it will get lost in the confusion of the debate. You can, however, answer some of the most important claims when it pertains to the issues that you are basing your campaign on. Keep your message constant and clear so that everyone understands what your positions are. Remember, stick with **your** theme. Again, do **not** try to answer and debate every little claim by your opponent. If you do, that is where all your energy will be spent. If you do not, the voters may very well consider you more professional in the way you handle yourself and may consider your opponent as a nit picker and someone they don't trust to lead their community. You can instill that feeling in the voter by telling the voters that you will not lower your standards for your campaign and that you will stick to the high road in the campaign and not get involved in mudslinging. You can do a phone survey and talk to twenty-five or more "good voters" to see which way the voters are responding to your campaign tactics as well as your opponent's, and adjust accordingly.

While literature and campaign signs are your most prevalent ways to get your message out, there are many other formats and ways to advertise. Let's touch on some of those now before we go on to the next chapter.

Bumper stickers are one of many ways to advertise. I don't like them, and in most cases, neither do the voters. They are hard to remove and can look unsightly. One only has to take a drive and check out the old half-scraped-off bumper stickers on the backs of vehicles. In my 1993 reelection campaign, I started using a suction cup triangle card. It looked just like the cards you have seen in people's back windows which say, "baby on board." They are cut square and the suction cup is affixed to the corner of the card through a hole punch and you hang it in the back or side windows and it looks more like a triangle than a square. These go over great with people because the triangles go inside the vehicle and do absolutely no damage. They can take it out and put it back in very easily and they don't cost any more than bumper stickers. Don't spend a lot on these, but as always, order what you feel you will need on the first order. It's always much cheaper to order 500 at once than to order 250 twice.

Billboards are very expensive and should only be used if you have more money than you need. Of course. that does not happen very often. I have only used them once, during my last reelection in 1997, and only because I had the extra money and decided to do it just to do it. In most cases, I would not recommend using them. Of course, if you are in a large city, you may need to use them.

There is a fairly new form of advertising that is quite affordable and effective. Go down to the local movie theater and ask if they run ads before each movie. Most large movie theater chains do this today. They usually contract with a company that does it for them. Find out who the contact person is and call them for the rates. I used this in my last reelection campaign and it was effective. My ad consisted of my picture and the wording "thanks for helping us make Westland *the place to be!*" It was worded that way because some theaters, the one in my city, for example, will not take political ads which ask for people to vote for a candidate. Check with your theater for their policy. If they do not allow political ads, try to put some other message up like the one I did, which did not actually ask for support yet still accomplished the same goal. If you are a real estate agent, you could advertise for that and you will get your face and name up, and if you are running for office at the same time it will accomplish your goal, getting you the recognition you need. If you are an incumbent officeholder, you can put up some type of message thanking the residents for making your community a great community, or another message which would not be political, yet accomplish the same goal. If you are just a resident, and they do not allow political ads, just put up your picture and say something like, "I am proud to be a part of this great community." My ad ran about eight times before each and every movie on every screen, every day. I paid just over one thousand dollars for a ten-week run. It was worth every penny. Even though it didn't ask people to vote for me, it was just as effective!

Newspaper ads are, in my opinion, not worth the money. I have never used them and probably never will. They cost too much and are not that effective, in my opinion. Some people don't share my opinion, so ask your inner circle to check the local rates and decide. You can find better things to spend your money on, though. Again, if you are in a large city, newspaper ads may be justified, but again, compare the cost and benefit against other forms of advertising.

Campaign pins are nice, but not necessarily the best form of advertising. I recommend that you buy some and give them out to friends and volunteers so that they can wear them while campaigning for you. Your volunteers will want something to show off and pins will keep them happy without you spending lots of money.

Hats and shirts are in the same category as pins. They are not the best value for your money, but again, your volunteers and friends will want something to show off or wear, so you should buy some. You don't need that many, just enough to keep your workers and friends supplied and happy. Make sure that when you give out hats and shirts, that you try to give them out to people who will wear them, although I admit that's not easy to do. There are a lot of hat collectors out there that will take the hat and never wear it. Use some common sense. Don't take fifty hats to a rally or a labeling party, because I guarantee that all fifty will disappear that night and you will be lucky if ten out of the fifty people wear the hat in public. A hat in someone's rack in their basement won't help you get elected.

Chapter Seven

Campaign Signs

Campaign signs are a very important part of any campaign. There are many ways to get your name out there and yard signs allow voters to show their support for you or maybe their opposition of your opponent. Campaign signs come in all sizes, shapes and colors. You need to design your sign, and the most important rule is this: **keep it simple!** Only put what is absolutely necessary on the sign, which means your name, office you're running for, a request to vote for you, and of course, your disclaimer. In both of my reelection campaigns, my signs read "reelect Thomas Mayor." You do not need your first or middle name on your sign unless someone with the same last name is on the ballot. I could have even made it simpler and had "Thomas" in the center of the sign using big letters and "Mayor" on the bottom in smaller letters. You can be sure that my next signs will be that way.

You will need to pick your sign crews, and when you do, you will need to train and instruct them as to how and how **not** to put up signs. Most of your sign crew people will work alone out of their car or truck, but if any of them want to team up, let them. Remember, they are volunteers and you need to keep them happy. Also, you need to select one person to be the "crew leader" of the sign crews. He will coordinate the work with the crews, assigning them their areas and making sure that everyone is doing it the way it is supposed to be done. Not only will the crew leader oversee the sign crews, he or she will drive around looking for such things as signs that are on rights-of-way, and move them, areas where you need more signs, and assisting any of the sign crews who need help. Your crew leader will also repair and replace signs when they need it. When your crew leader finds a sign crew that is not installing signs properly, he or she will need to get with that crew and retrain them, and I can assure you that will happen repeatedly.

You do not need to put City Council person, just put "Council." You do not have to put Township Trustee, just put "Trustee." Either put elect or reelect on the top, or nothing at all on the top, your last name in the middle and the office you're seeking at the bottom. Unless you are an incumbent, you will have to put the word "for" before the office you are seeking. Your name and the letters should be as big as the sign will allow. I have seen some campaign signs that have so much information on them that you could not possibly read it in the few seconds it takes to drive by it. Do not make that mistake. Again, keep it simple and it will be an effective sign.

You will need to decide how many signs you will need and what size you will want to use. As to the number of signs, it will vary greatly depending on the size of your community and on the amount of money you have to spend on signs. In a small community, you may only need fifty or one hundred signs. In a larger community, you may need anywhere from five hundred to three thousand or more. In my first campaign, I used about a thousand signs, and in both my reelection campaigns, I used about three thousand signs each. I could have used more in my first campaign, but money was limited and literature took priority over signs, so we spent what we could on signs. Also, make sure that you order extra signs, so that when some of your signs get soggy from rain or damaged from vandalism, you can just put a new sign cover on the wire. You will lose more signs than you will wires.

Now you will need to decide what size sign you will use. There are many shapes and sizes for signs. The shape of the sign will depend on your name to a certain degree. If you have a long name, you may want to use a single pole sign where your name is spelled out vertically or maybe an eleven by twenty-eight-inch sign, which is longer horizontally. If your name is fairly short, maybe five to seven letters, you probably will want to use a rectangle shape. My name has six letters and I use a rectangle shape. The sizes may vary from company to company, but most of them will have the basic shapes such as 5½ by 28, 11 by 14, 14 by 22, 11 by 28, 22 by 28, and 28 by 44 inches. Remember, you will want your name (last name) to be the largest and boldest letters on the sign. Longer names will require longer signs. You need to match your name to the size of the sign.

They will also offer larger signs such as 2 by 4 foot and 4 by 8 foot, but I would not recommend you use them unless you are running in a large city. They are expensive and hard to handle and they do not last as long as the smaller posters. These large ones do not hold up in the rain well. Most of these large signs are paper that you glue onto plywood, and when they get wet, you can be sure that you will have to repair them. If you do not get to them right away, the wind will rip the paper off and you will have to replace it. Another problem with these large signs is you will need a crew of at least two people and a pickup truck or trailer, post hole diggers, hammer and nails or screws and a cordless drill. There are some companies that sell these large signs in a stiff plastic material that is about a quarter-inch thick. These are waterproof and will hold up better, and if you wanted to use large signs, I would recommend you use these, but I would still give a lot of thought to using these large signs. The smaller signs will do the job! I have never used the large, wooden signs, with the paper sign material and I never will. I have never believed they were worth the money and the problems that accompany them.

You will also want to check local ordinances in your community to see if there are limitations on the sizes of political signs. Remember, it is your obligation to find out! Many communities have limits, and you want to know what they are **before** you order your signs. The limitations are usually on the large 4 by 8 signs, which can be a hazard. Some communities require you to pull a permit to put up political signs, and there are sometimes time limits as to when you can start and when you have to remove them. Some communities have a ban on political signs, although this is being contested in some courts.

There is usually an ordinance in most communities that makes it illegal to place any political signs on rights-of-way. You need to explain this to your sign crews so that they do not violate the ordinance. Rights-of-way can vary quite a bit from road to road, but you can use this as a rule of thumb. In a subdivision, the right-of-way usually ends about one foot in (towards the house) from the sidewalk. On major roads, you can use the sidewalk as a guide, but look for the light or telephone poles since they "should" always be on rights-of-way and place them at least six feet behind them, if possible. If you are unsure, just place the sign well beyond any utility pole or hydrant and it should be okay.

While your first priority is to place your signs in people's yards, you may need to place your signs on corners of main roads, even where there are empty lots. You are supposed to get permission from the property owner, but that is very difficult, and hardly anyone does that. Most every candidate will just put the sign up and if the owner complains, take it down. You can adopt a policy of only putting your sign up on empty corners or empty lots if your opponent does. This is a decision that you and your inner circle need to make. Maybe you will decide that you can afford the signs and you need the advantage. Keep in mind that there are some voters who don't like to see signs on empty lots or corners. Not all voters, just a certain percentage. Again, you will need to have your sign crew leader instruct your sign crews as to your policy on the installation of signs.

My advice is to use the smallest size sign that will fit most of your needs. They are cheaper to buy and easy to keep in the trunk of any car, even a compact one. I used three different size signs during all of my campaigns. I used a 14 by 22, 22 by 28 and a few 28 by 44-inch signs. I would not use the 28 by 44 ever again. They were more expensive and the wires used to put them up were over five dollars each, which is more than the cost of a few smaller poster signs. Plus, they were more difficult to install and they had to be carried on a truck or trailer. Sure, they were bigger, but when we placed a 22 by 28 next to it, you could see those almost as well. When you compare the cost of a 28 by 44 to the cost of a 22 by 28, you will find that you can buy two 22 by

28 signs for the cost of only one 28 by 44 sign. I would recommend that you use the smaller signs for as many of your locations as you can. Use the small ones for the front yards on subdivision streets. Do some experimentation with your signs by placing them in some yards and drive by them to see if they show good enough. Corner locations where the street comes out to a main road are great locations; get them whenever you can.

Also, have your sign crews place your sign closer to the house. This will save you a lot of time and money. Most people will put the sign just inside the sidewalk on the lawn. This makes it very enticing for a quick kick from someone walking down the sidewalk. Kids are great for this just to have something to do. Put them closer to the house. People will see the sign just as well as if it were next to the sidewalk. Remember, you are in a subdivision, and the people who live there will see it eventually, since they will drive by it every day. After awhile, you will know which size to put where. You will constantly need to train your volunteer sign crew people on where to place the sign as well as what size sign to use for each location. Signs are expensive and you can only buy so many. Make sure that they only put one in a yard. Some people ask for two. Also, if a homeowner asks for a few extras to give out to neighbors and friends, instruct your sign people to politely say that they just do not have any extra signs, because the supply is low. Tell them to ask the homeowner to give them the address of anyone who wants a sign, and then your sign crew can go and put it in. I can tell you that most of these extra signs your crew would hand out to people who ask for extras, will end up leaning against the wall in someone's garage. Believe it or not, just in the last week, I have had two people come into my office and drop off several signs each that they just had sitting in their garage!

As you begin to get sign locations, make the effort to create a sign list on the computer. You can use a program like Microsoft Access or Excel or any other off-the-shelf programs. You will want to be able to print out your list by precincts, wards or districts, whatever you have in your community. You can give these lists to your sign crews so that they know where to go, and the name of the voter whose yard they will be installing the sign in. You will build on this list as you go through the election that you are in, so make sure that you keep this list growing as you go along. As always, keep this list confidential. Your opponent will find out soon enough where your locations are, so no sense making his or her job any easier. The only person from the sign crew people who will need a full list of all sign locations is the crew leader. Do not give the complete list to any of the other sign crew people. Instruct your sign crews to knock on the door when placing yard signs just to make sure that it's still okay to put the sign in. If no one is home, they can put the sign in, but in any case, have them leave a flyer that I will explain at the end of this chapter, called—**"the care and feeding of your lawn sign."**

Do not put signs out too early and don't put them all out right away. You will want to start slowly, about eight weeks before the primary election, eight to ten weeks if there is only a general election. This is a general rule of thumb; your circumstances may warrant otherwise. Then, as the election date gets nearer, put more and more of them up. This is very important, do not peak too early. If you go out four weeks before the primary and put all of your signs up, you may find many of them destroyed or missing two weeks before the election, when you need them out the most. Save some of them for the last few weeks before the primary. Some candidates will use the method of waiting until their opponents begin to put up signs before they do. There is some merit to this method, however, if you are the newcomer and you're up against a strong incumbent, you cannot afford to wait too long. You may need to get your signs out and keep the pressure on your opponent. A strong incumbent will have enough money to blitz the town with thousands of his or her signs the last two or three weeks before the election.

Every candidate will deny vehemently that his or her supporters would ever stoop so low as to steal their opponent's campaign signs. Don't start out in the political world living in a dream world. You may as well face the fact that your opponent's supporters will steal some of your signs and your supporters will steal some of your opponent's signs, and there is nothing that you, or your opponent, can do about it. As a matter of fact, your opponent may use an old trick and literally have his own supporters "steal" or damage his or her own signs so that he or she can accuse you of masterminding this horrible crime against fair campaigning. Another trick your opponent may use is to have twenty or thirty of his or her supporters call for one of your campaign signs to be put in their yard and to request another one when it mysteriously disappears. Many campaigns have spent the last week with no signs to give out to their supporters, who are begging for them while hundreds of signs are sitting in the trunks of cars and in the garages of their opponent's supporters. Don't let this happen to you, pay attention and watch for this. You cannot prevent this totally, but you can keep it to a minimum if you watch for this. Remember, this is a game with no rules. Also, without telling anyone, you personally should hide a small amount of signs for the last week of both the primary and the general election as a backup supply. You can count on losing anywhere from ten to thirty percent of signs in most any campaign. Sometimes, it's just kids vandalizing them and weather taking its toll, but mostly, it will be vandalism by supporters of your opponent. You just have to live with this. **Do not** retaliate by having your opponent's signs removed or damaged, although even if you instruct your supporters not to do this, some of them will do it anyway. At least you can keep it to a minimum by telling them not to. It is not worth the bad publicity if you or one of your supporters are caught, and it does happen, and sometimes on camera! Just accept the fact that you will lose some of your signs and keep yourself focused on the campaign. If your opponent continues to make an issue out of his or her charge that you are stealing their signs and he or she is getting a lot of press coverage over it, try this tactic. Offer to pay for the replacement of twenty-five of them at three dollars each, which is about average. The press loves these kinds of stories because it will probably be the first time a candidate ever offered to do something like this in your community. Besides, where else can you buy that kind of PR for seventy-five dollars! The voters will respect you for it and your opponent will probably never take the money, anyway! And, it will probably shut your opponent up. Remember, you have to be smarter and slicker than your opponent!

Try to space your signs out in a neighborhood. Do not put them right next to each other unless you have enough money to buy a lot of signs. One or two signs per block will usually be plenty. If you have voters who demand to have a sign in their yard even though you may already have three or four on that street, then put the sign in. As with anything, use good judgment. However, if you are really limited in the amount of signs you have, you have to say no and spread your signs out around the community. By now, you can see how important money is to a campaign. You can never have enough.

There are a lot of places that you can order your yard signs from. You can either go to a local printer or a specialized company that deals in all types of campaign materials, such as signs, bumper stickers, pins, etc. While there are many local print shops who can make yard signs, I would recommend you use the local printer for such things as literature and stationery and use the specialized campaign shop for your yard signs, bumper stickers, pins, hats or whatever else you want. If there is not a specialized campaign sign company in your area, you may have to mail order your material. Pick one who has been in business for awhile and one who will give you references of candidates in your area that have used them. Take the time to check out those references. The only thing worse than not being able to buy any yard signs is to have ordered them and not get them in time for the election! At the end of this chapter, I have listed a few companies who specialize in campaign material. I am not inferring that these companies are good or reliable companies, I just list them for you as information. It is up to you to check up on any of them to see if you feel comfortable in dealing with them.

I can, however, give you a recommendation for one of these companies. Sawicki and Son, located in Detroit, Michigan, is the company that I have used for all my campaigns. They specialize in yard signs and all other types of campaign materials from chip clips to jar openers. They have been used by most of the candidates in my community and by many candidates in the Detroit metropolitan area. They are a great company. Their prices are reasonable and their quality of work is excellent. I would recommend that you call or write to them and get their catalog. They can supply you with signs that are completely assembled, partially assembled, or whatever way you want them. If you have to mail order your campaign materials, the key is to order early.

You can save some money by assembling your signs instead of having the sign company assemble them. I would recommend you have them assemble them if you can afford it. It usually costs as little as twenty-five cents per sign to have them completely assemble them. All you have to do then is stick them in the ground. You have many options. You can have them fold the signs and glue the sides, which leaves you with the job of stapling the signs to the wires by putting the sign over the wire and stapling the bottom to hold the sign on the wire. You will want to staple across the entire bottom of the sign to keep the wind from blowing it off the wire. If you are really stretched thin for money, you can fold them and staple the sides and staple the bottoms to hold them on the wire. The signs are usually printed two to a poster in reverse order so that when you fold it over, you have a double-sided sign. Be careful to use good staples for the signs. If you just try to use regular staples, they will keep coming apart. Go to a hardware store and find a hand stapler that uses undulated staples that are heavier than regular staples.

Also, when you order your signs, have them cut some of them into single posters. Some people will want to stick them up in the windows of their home. Some condo associations have a ban on political signs, but will allow window posters. The posters are also good to put up at the rallies and parties, especially election eve parties. Again, if you can afford it, have the sign company do the assembly, but if you do decide to do some assembly, get your sign crews together and make it a sign assembly party.

After the primary election, and, as always, surmising that you have won and are going on to the general election, you have another decision to make. Whether or not to pick up all of your signs and hold onto them for a few weeks before putting them back out for the general election. This will cut down on vandalism and normal wear and tear from the elements, but it will take a lot of work and coordination. I have never done this, but I know of candidates who do. I have always felt that leaving the signs up was a statement that we were in the race to stay and that we would not take a step back at anytime. I did, however, always lose a fair share of signs in the first week or two after the primary. You have to make your own choice, and again, money will play an important role in that decision. If you have enough money, I recommend that you leave them out there. Also, make up a half-sheet size flyer that you can title, "The care and feeding of your yard sign," that your sign crews can leave at the location of each yard sign. This flyer will explain things such as what to do if the sign is stolen or damaged, as well as how to remove and replace the sign when the grass is cut.

As I stated earlier, here are a few companies where you can order your campaign materials through the mail. Again, these are just a few, there are many more and I am sure there is one in your area if you take the time to check. You can call any of them and they will send you a catalog of their products. Except for Sawicki & Son, I cannot guarantee that the phone numbers or addresses are correct. I simply copied them down for you.

SAWICKI & SON
1521 W. Lafayette, Detroit, MI 48216
(313) 962-2725

ELECTION IDEAS COMPANY
127 W. Aurora Ave., Naperville, IL 60566
(800) 323-5656

PERSONAL SERVICE COMPANY
11970 ST. RT 37 North, Goreville, IL 62939
(618) 995-9393

There are many other companies that you can order your campaign materials from. I would suggest that you subscribe to a magazine called "Campaigns and Elections," located at 1414 22nd Street N.W., Washington, D.C. 20037. There is also a toll-free number available to order your subscription and back issues. It is 1-800-771-8252. This magazine has a great deal of information on elections. It also provides information on suppliers offering all types of materials and products for candidates. Actually, you should find at least one of the companies I just listed advertised in this magazine. These products range from political databases to campaign signs and bumper stickers. This magazine is usually available at your local bookstore.

This magazine also has numerous articles about how campaigns are run and they give a lot of examples of real campaigns that have actually happened. If you're interested in politics, you will find this magazine very interesting. They will also have articles that explain and show examples of how campaigns raise money, which is what chapter eight is all about. Read on!

Chapter Eight

Raising Campaign Money

Yes, it takes money to run for public office and you must be able to ask people to donate money to your campaign. And, not just your friends and family; you will need to ask complete strangers for money. If you cannot do this, you have a serious problem that will hurt your chances of winning any election, unless you are rich or have a rich relative. I recently read a quote in a Detroit area newspaper from Michael E. Duggan regarding campaign fund raising that I will always remember. Michael Duggan is the Deputy County Executive to Edward H. McNamara, the County Executive for Wayne County Michigan; and I might add, one of the best County Executives you will find anywhere. Michael's quote was—**"money is king."** He is absolutely correct!

The amount of money needed will vary greatly depending on a variety of factors including the size of your community, the office you are running for, and the make-up of your community. In my first campaign for Mayor, I raised and spent just over twenty thousand dollars, which is extremely low for a city of over eighty-five thousand people. In that race, my opponent was able to spend approximately one hundred thousand dollars. He was the incumbent Mayor and an incumbent is always able to raise more money no matter what the office is. The bottom line is that you need to raise as much money as you can. One way to get an estimate of the money you will need is to go down to the County Clerk's elections division and look up some of the campaign finance reports of people who have run for the same office you are seeking. Check both an incumbent and a non-incumbent to compare. Keep in mind that in order to look at someone else's campaign reports, you usually have to sign a card so that the person whose record you are looking at will know that you have checked their reports. For instance, if you are running for City Council, look up the reports of the candidates who ran for that office the last time, and look at the total amount of money they spent. This will give you a good idea of the amount of money you will need for your campaign.

To get started, hopefully you have stashed a little money away in anticipation of your campaign. As I said elsewhere in the book, you can usually **loan** your campaign money. This is wise to do since you can usually repay yourself later out of your fundraising. Make sure you fill out the proper paperwork when you do this, otherwise you may not be able to repay yourself. The next thing to do is to approach your family and friends. Your family can always pitch in some money for you and your friends will usually be willing to help out. Between your money and your family and friends' contributions, you can get your campaign off the ground and running. Keep in mind, there may be limits on individual contributions, so as always, make sure you check. Next, lean on your co-workers. Most of them will be excited to see someone they know run for office. Many of them have probably thought of running for office themselves but never seemed to take that first step and they will want to be involved in your campaign to see how it goes. Take whatever they will give you; five, ten, twenty, fifty dollars or more, it all helps. Of course, unless you have a rich aunt or uncle, your family, friends and co-workers will not usually be able to finance your entire campaign, so you will have to go elsewhere for the rest of your needed funds. You will have to put on fund raisers.

Pick a few of your inner circle to work directly on the fundraising committee along with a few other trusted volunteers. If you are a newcomer to politics, you don't have the name recognition like an incumbent, so you will have to start small with your fundraising. In my first election, I held two fund raisers before the primary election. One of them was a hot dog rally where I charged five dollars a person. For that, they got all the hot dogs and beer they desired. We invited everyone we knew and everyone they knew. We only raised a few thousand dollars, but it helped. Keep in mind that I put about five thousand dollars of my own money into the campaign to start. Hot dog rallies are a great way to get people together and to recruit volunteers to help with your campaign. If you happen to have a lot of campaign money to work with, you can throw *free* hot dog picnics at various locations in your community. They don't cost much and it's a good way to get people to come and sign up supporters. Make sure that if you throw *free* hot dog picnics, you invite **only** the people from your good voter list. Yes, this means invitations and postage, but remember, I'm only suggesting you do this if you have a lot of money. Whenever you have a fund raiser, have sign-up sheets for people to request a sign in their yard or to work on your campaign or to make a direct contribution.

Another good fund raiser is a cocktail reception. Even as a newcomer, you should be able to charge at least twenty or thirty dollars. For that, they get all the wine and cheese they can drink or eat. You can have the trays made up at a local supermarket or your volunteers can buy the cheese in large blocks and cut it up themselves. Wine is cheap if you shop around, so your profit on this type of fund raiser is excellent. There are other forms of fund raising such as breakfasts, golf outings, raffles or auctions. Some of these do not have a good profit margin, such as a golf outing, and some require getting licenses and permits from the state. Don't put on large dinners, people who attend these events don't expect it. Keep it simple with hot dog rallies, wine and cheese cocktail receptions and breakfast receptions. Talk to other people who have run for office before and they will be able to give you other ideas for fund raising, since there are many different ways to do it. Again, be careful. Raising money for political campaigns is different than raising funds for kids at school to go on a field trip. There are laws that govern the types of fund raising you can do and the process you have to follow, and remember, there are contribution limits in many states, and as I have repeatedly said, the rules can vary greatly from state to state. Make sure you assign one of your inner circle to research the restrictions and requirements for your state and community. Remember, if you make a mistake, you **will** read about it in the front page of your local newspaper!

When you have any fund raiser, make sure that you try to get around and talk to everyone who attends. I usually get there early and greet everyone who comes in and then I walk around to the tables and talk to people while they are eating. Do not sit down at one table and eat. Everyone else will wonder why you did not sit at **their** table. Remember, you are the candidate and everyone came to see you. The best way to get them to come to the next fund raiser is to say hi, thank them, and shake some hands. This brings me to an important piece of advice. Be friendly and use what I call the "touching method." I always make sure that I "touch" everyone I talk to. Maybe it's just a tap on the shoulder or back or a shake of the hand or putting your hand on their shoulder or elbow. It makes them feel like you care and that you are really glad to see them there. This is extremely effective!

You can generally rent halls at places like the Amvets or VFW. They are usually a good deal and they can supply you with bartenders and food quite reasonably. Check with municipal buildings also, since many of them have rooms for rent that may fit your needs. You can even have your fund raisers in a community park. Many of them have pavilions you can rent for under a hundred dollars and that can include using the grills. Some parks you can use for nothing! You should also consider having a fund raiser at your home, in your backyard or in the backyard of a friend or supporter. If you have enough money, you can rent a large hall or fancy banquet facility, but they can be expensive and many of them require you to use their caterers, and they are usually expensive. Remember, you are raising money for your campaign, not employing fancy caterers. Keep it simple! Contact the union groups in your community for support financially. Don't always assume that they will support the incumbent. In my first race against an incumbent Mayor, I was able to get the Police Officers Union, the Sergeants and Lieutenants Union, and the Department of Public Service Union to support me. They were unhappy with the Mayor and willing to take a chance on a newcomer. Make sure you contact these groups as soon as you decide to run. They may be willing to attend your fund raisers and you can sometimes get some large donations from these groups, especially the Police and Fire Unions.

There are a variety of ways to let people know about your fund raisers. Usually, you can send out a press release to the local newspaper and they will usually print a notice about your fund raiser for free. Remember, you are a candidate for office now and that makes you news. You can also have your volunteers put up flyers in restaurants or stores, but make sure they ask permission first. Some people simply do not want to get involved in politics by allowing a political flyer to be placed in their place of business, and you have to respect that. Have one of your volunteers contact some of the nonprofit groups such as the Rotary, Lions, Kiwanis clubs, etc., to inform them of your fund raisers. Generally, these groups do not endorse candidates, but they may attend your fund raisers and possibly ask you to speak before their group, and this is helpful as long as you can spare the time. Also, if you have been formulating a good list of supporters and sign locations, you can mail out notices of your fund raisers to them. Some of them will attend every one you throw! Some of your friends and supporters will volunteer to put notices up where they work. Use whatever method you can that doesn't cost you a lot of money. Putting an ad in the newspaper can be costly and may not be worth it unless you are running in a large community. Check out the rates and decide if it's worth it for your campaign. In any case, keep the cost of fund raising as low as you can so that the profit margin is as high as possible. You should be able to easily reach a ninety percent profit margin.

Another way to find people to invite to your fund raisers is to go down to the elections division and check out the campaign finance records of the incumbent candidate or candidates that you are running against. Many of the people who contribute to your opponent or other candidates in your community will also donate to your campaign. Many of these people are vendors, contractors and suppliers who do business with your community and they want to have some connection to anyone who may possibly be elected to any position in your community. Don't be shy about doing this. The smart candidate who wants to win will want every advantage he or she can get!

Chapter Nine

Endorsements

Endorsements come in many ways, but to use them without any problems, all or any endorsements should be in written form. You can get endorsements from individuals, groups and organizations, union groups, associations, etc. First, let's look at the necessity of endorsements. Everyone has a different opinion on the need for endorsements. Some say they are useless, and some say they are vital to any campaign. My opinion falls somewhere in the middle. I feel that if you can get the endorsement of a group or individual without too much effort or complication, then go ahead with it. If getting the endorsement will cost you something, and yes, many endorsements come at a political price, then you need to weigh the price against the usefulness of the endorsement. In many cases, the endorsement will not be worth the price.

Of course, there are many instances of groups or individuals who simply want to endorse your candidacy with nothing in return for it. Sometimes, they just dislike the other candidate. If that's the case and you do not have to go through some drawn-out process that takes a lot of your valuable time or carries any kind of political price, go ahead and secure the endorsement.

Let me explain why I say many endorsements are not worth the effort or the political price. In the past, endorsements were more valuable than they are today, and a way to secure the votes of the people who belong to a certain group or organization. This is not the case, today. People make up their own mind about who they are going to vote for, and even if their union or organization that they belong to requests that they vote for a particular candidate, they generally will not let that change their vote. If you don't believe this, try asking ten people if they let an endorsement change their vote. You may be surprised by how many of them will say no. So, even if you have the endorsement of a group, you may not receive very many votes from it. Remember what I talked about earlier regarding targeting voters? I will tell you time and time again throughout this book that it's *all in the numbers*.

Let's say for instance, a union in your community has a thousand members and they want to give you their endorsement. First, according to average statistics, only about one hundred and fifty of those thousand will actually vote in the local election that you are going to run in. Plus, how would you know that they **all** live in your community? If they did, however, out of that one hundred and fifty, some are going to support you for a variety of reasons such as: they don't like the other candidate, they always vote for the new person, or maybe they really like your message. Some of the one hundred and fifty will vote for the other candidate for some of the same reasons. What you need to understand is that there is a certain number of the one hundred and fifty that are undecided about who they are going to vote for. It is impossible to always know what that number is, but it could be as high as fifty percent. So, it could be that you are down to as little as seventy-five voters that **may** be swayed to vote for you because of the endorsement. Notice that I underlined in bold letters the word **may.** If you have to make some promise that compromises your integrity or the overall goals of your campaign, the endorsement may not be worth it. Remember, elections are all about numbers!

Also, endorsements can have a reverse effect. An endorsement from one group could cause people from another group to vote for your opponent. The two groups may be opposing one another for some reason that has nothing to do with you and you may be the one to suffer for it. You need to take into consideration a lot of issues before you agree to an endorsement. Don't take it just because it's offered.

That being said, if you decide to seek endorsements, here are some of the groups that you should contact. First and foremost, since you are running in a local election whether it's for Mayor, Council, Township supervisor, school board, Township trustee, county commissioner or other office, you should contact the employee groups that work for the community that you are going to be running in. The police and fire department unions are the most influential groups to deal with. They will donate both money and workers for your campaign, and in many cases, a lot of money. Then, contact other employee groups such as the union that represents the department of public service in your community and the union that represents the teachers and the maintenance workers for the school systems. There may also be a separate union representing the clerical workers of your community and you should contact them, also.

Most of these groups are involved in your community directly. They are usually quite knowledgeable about the political landscape that you are running in and they can be very helpful. They can donate large amounts of money and a lot of campaign workers to deliver literature, install signs and other such tasks. However, for those same reasons, they may request a lot in return for their support. In some cases, it might simply be just a promise to deal with them fairly, which is great. However, sometimes they want specific promises such as a minimum amount of raises for their next contract. Again, you need to weigh the political cost of the endorsement against the need for the support. If you feel that their support is absolutely necessary and you agree with their request, then by all means, do it. If you feel that you just cannot support their request, then you should politely withdraw your request for the endorsement. Meet with them and explain to them that you do not want to lie to them, but that you just cannot promise them what they want. Explain that you will always be fair and try to support them whenever you can. This may satisfy them and they may decide to support you simply because you have been honest with them. **Never lie to them or try to mislead them!** You need to establish a reputation of a person who is up front and honest about what they say and someone who will **do** what they say.

In my reelection campaign of 1993, I was walking door to door and I was stopped on the sidewalk by a man who said that he represented construction workers. He wanted to know if I would support a prevailing wage ordinance for our city. I told him that I would have to see exactly what kind of prevailing wage ordinance would be proposed before I could say for sure that I would support it as Mayor. He then told me that he was certain that my opponent would support a prevailing wage ordinance and that if I would not commit to doing the same, he would recommend to all the construction workers in my community to support my opponent. I explained that I would like to have their support but I would not lie to him to secure his support and the support of his membership. I told him that if a prevailing wage ordinance was proposed that I would look at it and as long as it would not cost the community a lot of money, I would support it. Well, he was not satisfied with that answer and he told me he was going to support my opponent. I apologized to him that I could not give him the answer he wanted and that maybe at some time in the future he would support me. After I won that election, I supported a new prevailing wage ordinance for our community in support of the construction unions. They respected the fact that I would not mislead them to secure their vote and yet still support their issue **after** the election. In my 1997 reelection campaign for Mayor, I had their support.

Next, go to other large employee groups in your community such as any factories or auto plants. They are usually represented by a union who will consider your candidacy. Many of the unions that represent large or medium factories have political action committees who screen candidates for every election. Their endorsement will sometimes come with a donation of money.

Endorsements take time and effort. If you are trying to get the endorsement of a group or union, you will most likely have to attend one of their meetings or screening committees. At these meetings, there will most likely be some disagreement about your endorsement. Do not be surprised if at the meeting you have some members asking you some tough questions and even making some nasty comments about you or your positions on labor issues or whatever issues that concern the group you are meeting with. Don't let this bother you. You should have conditioned yourself in the beginning of this venture with the knowledge that you would not please everybody. You should prepare some information about yourself and your candidacy for the meeting. Make at least a dozen copies to be passed out to the people running the meeting. If things get nasty at one of these screening committee meetings, and you don't see enough support to secure the endorsement, excuse yourself, get up and very politely explain that you do not wish to divide their group or cause any hardship, and remove your request for their endorsement. They will either apologize and get on with the screening or continue the debate. If they stop arguing and continue on, stay and try to secure the endorsement. If they continue to argue, take your leave and thank them for their consideration. If you feel that enough support is there, and it is just a small minority who is raising all the arguments, then stay and try to secure the endorsement. Use common sense.

Individual endorsements can be just as important to your campaign as the endorsement of a large group and sometimes even more so. Here's how you can use individual endorsements. You can ask residents to sign an endorsement sheet for your campaign. Use a sheet with maybe twenty or more signature lines on the sheet. Leave room for these individuals to put their address below their name. This way, you can send out a letter to the voters which ends by stating that "the individuals below all support my candidacy." The letter can even be written so that it is coming from all of the individuals who have signed it, instead of coming from you. If you make sure that you have at least one signature from each precinct, then what will happen is that many of the people who live in that precinct will recognize the signature as someone they know. Even if they don't know the person who signed your endorsement sheet, they will know that it is someone from their neighborhood and maybe that will swing their vote. Remember, some people will vote for you simply because one of their neighbors has your sign in their yard. So, collect those individual signatures for endorsement and arrange them so that your printer can take one or all of them and place them on any piece of literature. The really great thing about individual endorsements is that they generally come with no political price tag, except for a few individuals who may want an appointment if you get elected. If that happens, you simply need to decide if the endorsement of that individual is worth the price.

Here's how to get some free media using individual endorsements. Starting about three to four weeks before both the primary and general elections, get your supporters and friends to write letters to the editor about why they want to see you elected. Most local newspapers will print these in their editorial section. Make sure there is at least one in there every week and maybe two. Your inner circle can even draft some of the letters and hand them out to supporters and ask that they sign them and send them in. This is free advertising, and you can bet that your opponent will do this also. If not, you have the advantage. There are lots of ways to get free media. Calling press conferences to announce things that are happening in your campaign, or simply calling the local reporter to explain your position on any current issue. If something controversial happens at a public meeting, or residents are upset about something that is going on, call the reporter and explain your position on the issue or what you would do about that issue if elected. Your inner circle should make a list of ways to use the media without paying for it. Remember, you **are** the news when you are a candidate for public office.

Chapter Ten

Appearances at Events

You and your inner circle will have to decide which events you will attend. Some people will tell you that you should go to every event that you possibly can. I do not agree. You need to pick and choose carefully which events you go to. Remember, it's the numbers again. Your inner circle has to set some parameters that you use to decide whether or not to attend an event, such as when the event is, where it is, how many people will attend and where they are from. If there is an annual dinner for seniors in your community that is well attended, you should go. Seniors vote in a higher percentage. If it's a carnival that's attended by people from several communities, don't go. Most of the people will not know who you are and can't vote for you anyway. If the carnival is a community event put on by the community and attended mostly by people from your community, then go. If it's a craft show at the mall, don't bother. Get the idea. You need to keep in mind whether or not the event is attended by enough people who can vote for you. If not, you are better off walking through a neighborhood knocking on doors of people that you know **will** vote.

You may get a request to go and visit at a church in your community. This is usually a good use of your time. You will be seen by a few hundred people in a short amount of time and most of them will probably live in your community. It's usually early in the morning, which is not a good time for door knocking, anyway. You could always start out Sunday with a stop at a local church, have some lunch and then go door knocking from say one to five p.m.

As I said earlier in the book, coffee hours are usually not a good use of your time. If you do them, try to make sure to schedule them for times that are not good for door knocking, like Sunday mornings or even Sunday evenings. Again, those are not good times for door knocking. Do not trade a premium evening from five to eight p.m. to go to a coffee hour to see ten people, out of which only two will vote. Remember, it's the numbers.

Candidate forums, which are put on by many different groups, are designed exclusively for the purpose of introducing each candidate to the voting public on an equal basis. These are usually good to go to since you will be seen by voters in your community. One problem with these types of events is they usually have a light turnout. These forums are put on by such groups as the Rotary, Lions Club, Democratic and Republican clubs, union groups, chambers of commerce, etc. Beware though, the group putting on the event may be supportive of your opponent and may be attempting to set you up for a fall. They could be loading the audience with their supporters and even loading the panel who screen the questions for the candidates so that you get all controversial questions and your opponent gets questions that are easy to answer or designed to highlight your opponent's strong points, and yes, this really does happen. In my first campaign in 1989, I was invited to a debate sponsored by a large community group. Neither I nor any of my campaign team knew any of the rules up until about ten minutes before the start of the debate. Not one person friendly to my campaign was involved in screening the questions that we were to answer. It was all handled by supporters of my opponent. We were so prepared for the debate, however, that we won easily. This was my second debate of my first election and I had learned the importance of being prepared from the experience I had with my first debate that I will tell you about in the next few pages.

Make sure that if you attend candidate forums that you ask questions about who will be involved in what, what are the rules of the forum, such as the time allotted to answer questions, and whether or not there is any rebuttal to answers. Do some research into the group sponsoring the event. If you are not comfortable with the rules and the answers you receive, do not hesitate to request changes in the rules or procedures. Do this in writing and request written responses to your questions. I have done this myself, especially in my reelection campaign in 1997. This will keep the forums as fair as possible. If they refuse to accommodate your requests or give written responses, that is your first clue that you may be in trouble. If you have a written trail of your questions and requests, you can defend your position of not attending, to the public and to the media. The group putting on the event usually will not want to look as if they are not being fair and easy to work with, so you can usually get them to make some changes, but **you** have to take the initiative. Once you have decided to attend the event, make sure that you get as many of your friends, family and supporters to be in the audience. Make sure that they submit questions to the panel if that is the format. Most of all, be prepared. Some of these forums are very simple with as little as five or six questions that are posed to each candidate, and some even give the list of questions to each candidate before the event. However, some of them are very intense, with many questions being asked that you may not be prepared to answer. Some candidate forums are full-fledged debates. Sometimes, there will be a debate before the primary election, but in most cases, the debates will usually take place after the primary has narrowed the field of candidates and the winners of the primary go on to face each other in the general election. Treat debates the same way as you treat candidate forums, but you will need to actually practice the art of political debating. Here's how to prepare and practice.

First, make a written list of every possible question that you think anyone might ask you about the campaign or your candidacy. Then, use someone's basement and set it up as if it were a real debate. You will want a table for you, one for your opponent or opponents and some chairs for the audience. If you can, get a sound system with three microphones and hook them up. One for you, one for your opponent or opponents and one for the audience. Then, get some of your inner circle, family and friends to ask you questions just like it was a real debate and have one or more of your inner circle "play" your opponent. Your inner circle can take turns being your opponent. Have the "audience" ask you any questions they want, including the ones you have written out. Have someone write down the questions that your "audience" asks and add them to your list. If your answers are not quick and correct, keep practicing until they are. You will find that if you do this several times for a couple of hours each time, you will become very adept at answering pop questions. If your answers are wrong, or just don't sound right, you will have the luxury of going over and over your answer with your inner circle to make sure that you eventually get it right. At the "real" debate, if you screw up an answer, you may not get a second chance.

You can also practice your rebuttals to your opponent's answers. When you make a list of questions that you think someone might ask you during the debate, try to guess what your opponent's answers will be. Then, formulate your responses to his or her answers. You should make yourself up a "fact book." You can do this by putting some stick-on tabs on a large spiral bound notebook. Write the issues on the tabs, and on the pages write the questions and your responses as well as your opponent's position and your responses to your opponent's positions. This way, no matter what issue is brought up or what question is posed, you can select the proper tab, open the spiral book and you will have the answers and possible responses of several questions on any given issue available to you at your fingertips. You will have to abbreviate your written material as much as possible. Sometimes, just a few "key words" will be all that is necessary to formulate your responses if you practice like I explained. This is very effective, and most candidates will not be this prepared. The fact that you are will make you look as though you are the better candidate. I was once so prepared for a Mayoral debate that my opponent complained that I was reading notes during the debate. Of course, when my turn came for a response, I told the audience that I was not going to apologize for being prepared for the debate by having done my research and having the information at my fingertips. I explained that I have always prepared for whatever I was going to do and that if they elected me as their Mayor, I promised to be "prepared" to take on the task. You have to be slicker than your opponent. Remember, this is a show and you are the actor.

Again, the most important thing when attending forums and candidate debates, is to be prepared and to ask questions about the rules and procedures. If you go into any of these blindly, you are just asking for trouble. If you think every group who puts on these forums and debates are always going to treat you fairly, then go outside, grab a two by four and whack yourself in the head a few times and then come back in and continue reading the book. I can vividly remember my first experience with debates when I was invited to a candidate forum by a very respected Chamber of Commerce. I had a letter which clearly stated that I had a ten-minute time slot to speak, and if I wanted to answer any questions, that would be up to me. However, when I arrived, I discovered that this was a full-fledged Mayoral debate which was televised on cable television. This turned out to be my *first* debate that I mentioned a few pages ago. I had no material for a debate, was totally unprepared and all alone, and had no support group in attendance. The audience was made up of the Chamber members and my opponent's staff and supporters. Keep in mind that my opponent was the incumbent Mayor at the time. I was also told that my opening remarks were reduced from ten to only five minutes. I found myself in the bathroom trying to decide what to do with my situation. I had only ten minutes to reduce a ten-minute speech to five minutes, and then face my opponent in a televised debate with absolutely no materials and not even one person in the audience who supported me. This wasn't a debate, it was a roast and I got roasted! The unexpected thing is that I survived the debate and even gained a little respect from some of the audience for hanging in there under these circumstances. Most thought I would fold up under the pressure. Of course, that didn't happen, but it goes to show you that you cannot take anything for granted. It's your job to ask the questions and get written responses before the event so that you will know what is taking place. If you don't, it just might be your turn in the oven!

Chapter Eleven

Cable Television and Commercials

The decision whether or not to use cable television to promote your candidacy is usually based on how much money you have. If you have the money, go for it. Regular television is usually too expensive for candidates for local races, except in the largest of cities, such as Detroit or Seattle. In cities of that size, candidates can usually afford regular television rates, although even in large cities, cable is much cheaper, and a great bargain. In the average size communities, local cable is the answer and is being used more and more every day by local candidates. You may be in a very small community that doesn't have cable, and in that case, you probably won't need it anyway. If you have cable in your community, they should have an office that you can contact regarding the rates for political advertising on the local channel in your community, as well as the rates for commercial time on such channels as CNN, ESPN, AMC, the Discovery Channel, the History Channel and many more. The rates for political advertising are usually the lowest rates they have ever charged for the time you are asking for, and believe me, the rates for local cable are a great deal. I live in a city of eighty-five thousand people and I have paid as little as five dollars for a thirty-second commercial spot on channels like CNN, ESPN and the Family Channel. I have paid as little as five dollars for an hour of air time on the local channel, which is a channel that is usually dedicated to each community by the cable company.

Here is a piece of advice for you incumbents. If you have cable in your community, you probably will have a government channel that is dedicated to your community. Many communities will use this channel to show public meetings such as council meetings, school board meetings and the like. In some communities, the school system will have its own channel. No matter what office you hold, you should have some opportunities to get yourself on one of these cable channels which is watched by many of the residents and you would be surprised by just how many! Make sure that you get on it as often as you can. It's free air time; and it is one advantage that you will always have over the challenger. And, it is perfectly legal and proper for you to be on there as long as you are not asking people to vote for you.

You can use cable for either commercials or even programs that run either a half-hour or a whole hour. The biggest cost of doing commercials or political programs on cable is the use of the studio time to put the commercial together or to film the program. If you have someone who has the equipment necessary to film your material and make it studio-ready, so that you can purchase the air time and just supply the tapes to the cable company, you will save a tremendous amount of money. You generally cannot use home equipment for this. You will need commercial equipment that is usually referred to as industrial equipment, and uses three-quarter-inch tapes instead of standard half-inch tape. There are new digital camcorders and Hi-eight equipment available at your local electronics store that you may be able to use to tape your own shows or commercials. One of your supporters may even have this type of equipment. Make sure that you talk with someone at the studio of the cable company to see if they will be able to run your own tapes before you purchase any equipment. In most cases, you will be better off having someone who has the commercial equipment do the taping of your shows.

I have never used cable air time in the primary, only in the general. My reasoning for that was to save the expense and the use of the air time for the general election, when the field of candidates was narrowed down, and to use the surprise factor which I will speak of later. In my runs for Mayor, there were as many as six candidates in the primary and only two in the general. In a Council or other type of race, where there are as many as four slots open, there could be as many as twenty candidates in the primary, and that would be narrowed down to only eight candidates for the general. By using cable air time in the general, you get to focus on fewer opponents and you can spend more time getting your message across.

I have used both commercials and political programs for my campaigns. The commercials are great and they get your face and name on the air at all times of the day and night. I have also used one-hour time slots for my campaign and these were very, very effective, yet a lot of people still do not use this method. Let me explain how we used them.

You can buy half-hour or full-hour time slots on the local channel. As I said before, I have paid as little as five dollars and as much as seventy-five dollars for an hour, depending on the time slot. It averaged out to about thirty dollars an hour because we selected time slots at two or three in the morning. Yes, people are watching at this late hour and they will watch candidates who are running for office in their community. What we set up was a paid political program where we set up two nice padded chairs with a coffee table in the middle. I would sit in one chair and my interviewer would sit in the other. My interviewer would ask me questions about the campaign and about the various issues regarding the campaign and my opponent. The great thing is that you already know what the questions are going to be since you will be the one to write the questions and you can take all the time you need to go into detail about the issue. You cannot do that in a thirty-second commercial. These programs were a huge success. The first time we did it, everyone in town was talking about the program. Since I was able to explain everything in detail, my opponent was totally surprised and could not respond to all of it in the limited space available on literature and it was too late in the game for my opponent to put a similar show like that together to respond in kind. That's another reason to wait until the general election to do this. The surprise factor alone is worth it. We always had the shows air the last three weeks of the campaign, and we kept it secret so that no one knew we were doing it. In my last campaign, I did the one-hour political interview from the living room of my home, and I selected the teacher of the year in my community for 1997, Ms. Vickie Sorensen, to interview me. The show went fantastic and the home scene had such a warm touch to it with the fireplace lit up in the background. Since Vickie was such a popular and well-known teacher in our community, the show was watched by almost everyone in town.

These one-hour paid political shows are dynamite, and if you can find the money to do them, do it. They are extremely effective and even more so if you can keep your opponent from finding out until the last minute. Just think how **you** would feel, if in the last three weeks before general election day, you saw your opponent on cable television eight times a day for a whole hour each time, explaining what he or she will do for the community if elected. Then, think how you would feel if there wasn't enough time to respond with a show of your own. You would feel as if the political rug had just been pulled out from under you. Well, that's exactly how your opponent will feel if you are the one who shows up on cable television. It will also take a little wind out of the sails of your opponent's supporters, at a most critical time, when they watch you on television going into detail on how you are the better candidate! Again, timing is important. Do not air the show until the last two or three weeks, so that your opponent doesn't have time to set up his or her own show. Remember, it takes time to put the show together and the cable company has to have time to put the show into the programming schedule, so get it done early. Remember, keep it a secret and use this surprise factor to your advantage, it works!

Political commercials on cable or regular television can also be a great way to get you the name recognition you need. These are just thirty- or sixty-second spots, so the message is quite limited. There are hundreds, if not millions, of ways to do commercials on cable or regular television, so I will not even try to explain them all; that would fill an entire book by itself. My advice is to keep the message short and to the point. If you try to cram a lot of information into a thirty-second spot, it may not hit home with the voter. Stick with your major issues that you have used throughout your entire campaign. Sit down with your inner circle to decide what you want to accomplish with your commercials. If you just want to get your face and name out there, your commercial may simply consist of a shot of you asking the voters for their support on election day. If you want to talk about your opponent, you will not want to show your face until the last few seconds of the commercial, with a request for support of your candidacy. Never show your face or name when the commercial is portraying your opponent in a negative light and only use negative ads when you feel them absolutely necessary, and then do them as professional as you can. You may want to do some comedy in your commercial and those are very effective. In my 1993 reelection campaign for Mayor, I used a mime that simply turned the pages of a large easel pad that had a message that basically requested the voters to support me on election day. Again, there are many ways you can do these commercials and you need to decide what is right for you, your campaign, and your community. Of course, your funds may be limited and maybe you will not be able to afford cable time, but if you can do it at all, I would recommend the hour-long programs first, and then if you can, do some commercials.

If you cannot afford to do any commercials or shows to be aired on cable, there is another alternative that you can do on either a small, medium or large scale, depending on your finances. You can use home equipment to tape a ten- or fifteen-minute program with just a head shot of you talking about your candidacy. Don't go over fifteen minutes because most people will get bored with watching a head shot of someone talking. I would recommend using a Hi-eight or digital camcorder to tape it and you can set the camcorder on a tripod. I am sure that one of your supporters will have this equipment if you don't. Talk about the important issues of your campaign and tell the voters what you will do for them if they elect you. Once you are certain that you have a good ten- or fifteen-minute tape of yourself, you can set up some regular half-inch VCR's and make some copies of your tape. That is the reason for taping the original with Hi-eight or digital equipment. Your copies will turn out better than if you tape with just standard half-inch tape. Make as many copies as you can afford. There are companies out there that specialize in making copies at a pretty low price, check those out.

Once you have them, here is what you can do with them. You can mail or hand deliver a copy of this tape to the homes of the "good voters" where there are at least three or more "good voters" in the household. Since you are doing this because you can't afford to use cable, you will have a limited amount of copies and you can't waste them on single-voter households. At the end of your tape, explain to the voter that your finances are limited and that you would like them to do you a favor by handing this tape over to a neighbor or friend who they think will vote in the election. Some people will actually do this for you and pass the tape off to someone else, which helps you get maximum use of your homemade tape. One word of caution. Make sure that the end copy that you deliver looks good. Use back lighting to make sure that there are no shadows and use a good microphone even if you have to rent or borrow one. Also, if you have created a fairly good video, your local cable company may have a public access channel available for free. You need to check to find out. Usually, you have to be trained on how to use the equipment, but if you're not, try to find someone who is trained and belongs to the group that uses the public access channel. Ask them if they would put the tape on. Maybe you can even find someone in the public access group that will do an interview. Keep in mind that the public access channel is not watched by a large audience, but it is better than nothing. These are not the best methods of getting on the airways, but if money is limited, and you have no other alternative, give it a shot, and try to make it look as good as you can. The only drawback is that if the tape you create is sloppy or too unprofessional looking, it could actually hurt you instead of help you, so be careful.

While we're on this subject, let me give you some suggestions on how to handle the news media. If you are in a large community of say two to three hundred thousand people or so, you will have some of the major news stations who will interview you on television and radio. Use all the air time you can get and try to get your message across to the voters. Be careful of your responses because most of this is live and cannot be changed once it's done. You only get one shot for your answer and you can be sure that if the reporter can surprise you with an unexpected question, and get an unprepared response from you that may

89

not sound good, that's what you will see on the nightly news, and they will not be interested in allowing you to respond to clarify your answer because they will be on to the next story, and quite frankly, they could care less.

Never, and I repeat, **never,** think that a news reporter is your friend, or is going to portray you in a good light. That is not their goal. Their mission is to sell news and newspapers. As we all know, good news and nice stories **do not** sell. Controversial and bad news **does** sell, and that's what reporters want, and if they can create it or foster it, most of them, not all, will.

Be cautious when dealing with the local news reporters. If you live in an average size community or a smaller one, you will most likely be dealing with one or two small, local papers. They will cover the campaign and do stories on all the candidates. You should make contact with someone at your local papers and give them a written copy of your position on the major issues of the campaign. Make sure they have a phone number where you can be reached because they will call you when your opponent makes a claim concerning you or your campaign. Usually, they will want to get positions from all the candidates. **Do not** expect to always see exactly what your response was in the paper, it will not happen. You might do a half-hour interview and go into detail about an issue and you will see just a few comments in print, and they may not be the comments that you wanted them to print. Give them short answers and try to be concise. Let me give you an example of how reporters can turn a story on you.

Let's say that a reporter asks you to respond to something your opponent said about you and let's say that this is your response, "Well, I think my opponent has his opinion on the issue and I have mine. We have discussed most of the issues in this campaign in a professional manner and I have enjoyed the give and take between us, and while most of our discussions have been polite and professional, I think that he's being a little childish over this one issue." What you very likely will see in the front page of the paper in big, bold letters for a headline is, *candidate A calls candidate B--childish!* This sells newspapers. They may not even mention the positive things you said about your opponent. You can call the reporter and complain and explain about all the other things you said and ask for a clarification, but if you get it, it will not be on the front page in big, bold letters. It will be on page ten in some corner in small print where no one will see it. That's just the way newspapers operate. Get used to it and be careful. Don't just run off at the mouth every time a news reporter comes up and starts asking you questions. Think before you speak and don't be afraid to tell them that you will have to call them later with an answer. They are used to that.

Most local papers will do a special edition before both the primary and general election showing all the candidates and their responses to several questions. Be sure to participate in these when they become available. You will need a stock campaign photo for this and all your literature, however, sometimes the papers will want to take your photo when you go in for the interview. Make sure you look professional, but relaxed. Don't hesitate to ask them to take another angle if you do not like the first photo. Usually, they will oblige.

Never think that newspapers are not political, because they are. Never believe that they are not biased, because they are. They, like everyone else in the world, have an opinion. They will favor one candidate over the other and you will see it in how they handle the stories about the different candidates. You just need to cross your fingers and hope that you are the candidate that they favor. Most local papers will endorse certain candidates for each office. Some will do endorsements in both the primary and the general, but many will do them only in the general. That endorsement may help convince the voters who have not made up their minds yet, so you need to try to convince the local papers that you are the best choice. Sometimes, however, no matter what you do, no matter how convincing you are, you cannot convince them, because they have already made up their minds. I have discovered over the years that unless an incumbent has really screwed up, or the newcomer has something very unique or special about him or her, the papers will usually endorse the incumbent. Don't lose any sleep over it, just keep working on your campaign and stay on course; it's not the worst thing in the world. Many people have won races without **any** endorsements from the papers. I am one of these people. When I first ran for Mayor in 1989, my opponent was endorsed by both local papers, and I still won. If you do get the endorsement, you can take the endorsement article to your printer and they can make flyers out of them and you can pass them door to door at the last minute. This will sometimes help convince some of the people who have not made up their mind yet.

Chapter Twelve

Primary Election Day

Okay, the big day is here and you have done everything that you were supposed to, and more. Your literature was mailed out on time and all your yard signs are up. You have been knocking on all the doors you possibly could and making sure that you targeted your voters carefully. You mailed out a letter to the absentee voters. You attended all the important functions and candidate forums. You conducted your interviews with the local papers and had your supporters drive their cars and trucks around town with your signs in the side and back windows. There is really nothing more that you can do but wait for the numbers to come in.

Let's talk about what you need to do for election day. First, if the other candidates are going to use poll workers, then you should use them, also. Poll workers are volunteers who stand at the voting precincts and hand out a card with your picture on it and ask the voters who show up to vote in support of you. Some poll workers will hand out pencils, rulers, yardsticks and all sorts of campaign material. Make sure your volunteers know the rules regarding the handing out of these materials. There are other rules regarding poll workers and your volunteers need to know all of them.

There is much debate about the value and the usefulness of poll workers. Some people believe that most people have made up their mind when they come to the polls and some think that the percentage of people who still have not made up their mind is substantially high. I don't think anyone knows the answer for sure. I believe that it can vary greatly from community to community and election to election. It can vary because of different candidates or many other reasons. The bottom line and the rule of thumb I use is that if the other candidates are using them, I use them. If my supporter gets to the polls and my opponent does not have anyone working the poll, I tell my poll workers to relax, greet people who come in to vote, or go to another poll and see if my opponent has anyone working there. If you have an abundance of volunteers who want to work the polls, then by all means, let them do so, even if your opponent doesn't have any out working the polls. Most candidates do not have an abundance of volunteers, so you have to learn to use them wisely. You may want to assign a few volunteers who will work out the schedule of poll workers if you are going to use them.

If you use poll workers, you will need to supply what is called "coffee wagons." You need to ask your volunteers who have vans or trucks to drive around to the precincts and hand out hot coffee, pop, and sandwiches or hamburgers to your poll workers. You can usually get someone like McDonald's, Hot and Now, or a local restaurant to supply the coffee. If they can't supply the insulated jugs, you can go to places like Sam's Club, and get the large five-gallon insulated jugs for coffee. That's a good place to buy the pop, also. Make sure that you rinse the coffee jugs out thoroughly or the coffee will taste like plastic. For sandwiches, I recommend that you go and meet the manager of either a Hot and Now or McDonald's to supply you with burgers. Don't mess with fries and chips and all kinds of stuff. It can become a problem. Just give them something hot or cold to drink and something to eat.

Some candidates will want to place yard signs around the polling places. Check the rules regarding this with the Clerk's office and with the polling place. Many times, the polls are at public schools or churches and they may have some rules you need to follow, but the Clerk can let you know what you need to do. If there is a disagreement about an issue and the schools are telling you one thing and the Clerk is telling you something different, listen to the Clerk.

Whether or not you use poll workers, you as the candidate, can and should go around and visit the different polls on election day. Stop at each poll for a few minutes or so and talk to the voters coming in to vote. Voters like to see the candidates on election day. Also, if you do use poll workers, you need your best volunteers to stay at the poll until it closes, and go inside for the reading of the machines. Your volunteer should be able to get the number of votes cast for each candidate from the election workers right after the last vote is cast. If you don't have poll workers, you can either assign volunteers to go to each precinct at the close, which is usually eight p.m., or you can have some stationed at the Clerk's office to get the reading of the numbers.

You should have someone create a "vote board" that you can hang on the wall with the names of the candidates, and a box for each precinct, so that you can put the amount of votes for each candidate in the box for each precinct. I have created a sample of a vote board below that you can use as a guide. You can go to an office supply store and get poster board and a thick black marker to make one up. It's cheap and simple. This can be the most exciting part of the evening, unless you are losing, then it can be very depressing. Of course, you should be prepared for either. As you can see, I have put six precincts up so that the number of votes cast for each candidate can be listed in those precincts. Of course, the size and population of your community will determine how many precincts, wards or districts you will have.

Candidate	1	2	3	4	5	6	Absentee	Total
Clark	143	77	211	346	37	72	660	1546
Doe	156	78	220	332	28	63	546	1423
Jones	189	89	243	321	41	57	212	1152

You need to make arrangements to have a place to have the primary results party. This could be at someone's house, your house, a restaurant, or a small hall that you can rent for a small fee. It's nice to have some beer, pop and wine and just some chips and pretzels there for your friends and supporters to munch on while waiting for the numbers.

This will be the most stressful time for you as you wait for the first numbers to come in. You will be wondering if you have done everything you could to win, and you will have lots of second thoughts and doubts, but just stand tall and confident and don't let your supporters know that you are thinking about any of that. Be prepared for any outcome. If you lose, be proud and thank all of your supporters for all of their help. Then go home, get a good night's rest and know that you have done what many people only talk about doing. The experience alone is well worth what you have been through. Get up the next day and get on with your life, and somewhere along the way, you will decide if you will try it again or not. Either way, you can and should be proud of what you did.

However, if you win, and if you have followed the guidance in this book, your chances are extremely good, you can celebrate the victory with all your friends and supporters until the wee hours of the night. Don't be too surprised if you find that before the night's out, you will have many friends and supporters at your party that you have never seen before. It is amazing how fast they can show up once you have proven your ability to win, especially if you had a very strong showing in the primary. In my 1997 primary race for Mayor, I came in very strong with sixty-eight percent of the vote. I will never forget the councilman, who had been quite stand-offish up to then, that showed up during the results and ended up with a "Thomas for Mayor button" pinned to his shirt. He was not wearing it when he came in! However, he was wearing one **after** the results came in!

Remember, I told you that elections are all about numbers. Well, now you have some real numbers to look at. You will see how many votes you and your opponent or opponents got in each precinct. These numbers are very important and they tell an important story. You need to sit down and study the results in great detail. I would suggest that you make copies of the vote board and tape them to your wall in your living room or your basement so that you see them every day as you go on to the general election. In my first election for Mayor in 1989, I taped the vote count poster boards in my living room. They took up three walls and I looked at them every morning and every evening. They were constantly on my mind and every time I looked up at them, I was wondering why people voted the way they did in each precinct and it helped me to develop a strategy on which precincts I needed to work harder in. **You must study these primary results thoroughly!** And, not just your results. You need to study the results of your opponent or opponents to see what area or precincts he or she may be weak in. These results tell an important story and you need to know just what that story is. If you lost a precinct, there is a reason for it and you need to find out. If your opponent is strong in a certain precinct, there is a reason for that. Again, you need to find out why. I cannot stress to you just how critical and important this is.

You need to determine what happened in each precinct. You need to be smarter than your opponent. If you lost a precinct by a good margin, try to find out why. Have some volunteers do some phone calls to the voters in that precinct and ask people why they voted the way they did. Maybe they are upset about your position on an issue that affects them greatly. Once you know, maybe you can make an adjustment of your position and for sure, you can do some extra work in that precinct. If you cannot change your position, at least you can explain why and still try to convince the voters that you are the right choice. If you won a precinct by a large margin, while there is never a guarantee, you can be fairly certain that you will win that precinct in the general and maybe you will not have to work as hard in that precinct. As you go through and study all of the precincts, you will easily spot the precincts that you need to put extra work into. Concentrate on those precincts but do not forget the other precincts. You are still going to have to work in the ones you won, but you will be able to put more effort into the ones that you were not strong in. This is one of the best things about a primary. You get to see how you are doing in the race and you get a chance to adjust your strategy for the general election.

Reading and comparing the election result numbers will be easier if you are running for an office such as Mayor or township supervisor, since there will be fewer candidates in the primary and only two candidates in the general election. In contrast, if you are running for city council, school board or township trustee, or similar office, there could be quite a few candidates in the primary, sometimes as many as thirty or more. Even in the general election, there will be generally double the number of positions that are open. For example, if there are four seats open in a city council race, generally there are eight candidates running in the general election.

If you are running in this type of race (city council, school board, township trustee, etc.), you need to be a little more cautious about your conclusions while reading the numbers from the election results in the primary. You may have come in first in the primary election and now think that you have it made going into the general. **Think again!** Have you forgotten that two by four lesson I told you about earlier? I have seen people come in first place in the primary race for city council and then come in dead last in the general election. Running for an office that has more than one seat open is very different than running for an office that has several seats open. Think about this. If you were running in a school board election which has four seats open, and everyone who comes to vote can vote for only four people, and you come in first, how do you know that you weren't simply everyone's last choice. This **can** and **has** happened. The lesson to be learned here is while you need to study the numbers to see what areas or precincts you need to work harder in, do not let the primary numbers convince you that you are the front-runner and that you can take it easy. If you don't believe me, just check some of the previous races in your community or surrounding communities. I'll bet you will find a race or two where one candidate won the primary by a landslide only to come in last in the general election. This can easily happen in races where there are more than one seat up for grabs in the general election. If you are an incumbent running for reelection in a race where there is more than one seat open, and you came in first in your last election, don't just assume that you will come in first in your reelection. You may have been everyone's "last" choice in the previous election. That is why you can't take things for granted, especially in elections where there is more than one seat up for grabs!

Chapter Thirteen

Phone Banks and Surveys

By now, you have taken the time to study the primary results and you now know where you are strong and where you are weak. Of course, you may have found that you are weak in every precinct, but at least you made it. If you are a Mayoral candidate or a candidate for Township Supervisor or Clerk, etc., there are only two of you left and it is easier to compare the results. If you are running for School Board, City Council, Township Trustee, County Commissioner, etc., then comparing the numbers will be a little more difficult since there could be anywhere from five to eighteen people or more left in the race, depending on how many positions are available. In some counties there are nine positions for County Commissioner. In most communities, there are either five, seven or nine City Council positions, although remember, it is a rare case when all the positions are open at one time. In my community, which has a Council made up of seven people, four Council positions are open every two years.

Even though there may be several candidates left in the race that you are in, you still should look at **your** numbers carefully. Once you have, you need to set up a small group of supporters to do some phone surveys. I would recommend you use your inner circle if they are not too busy doing other things. They can actually do it from their own homes or you may have a location available to you that has several phone lines. Either way works fine. I always split up the lists of people to be called and gave them to several people and let them work from their homes. You will need to call only the "good voters" in the precincts that you are checking on. Have your people ask why they voted the way they did, and ask them if they had any specific problem with you as a candidate. Maybe they just didn't know much about you, or maybe they never received any literature from you, or maybe they just do not want change at this time. When they make a contact with someone who voted for you, have your callers ask why. Make sure that your people are very courteous on the phone. Have them finish the conversation by asking the voters to at least listen to your views and read your literature to give you a fair chance to try to win them over. Voters like this attention; it makes them feel as if you really care about them and want them to be involved in the process.

Let's say that you came in strong in the primary and won every precinct in your community. Great! Now you can head out to the movies and not work extra in any precinct, right? **Wrong!** That kind of thinking has lost more elections than you would ever imagine. As I said earlier, I know of people who were the top vote-getters in the primary and at the bottom in the general. This can be especially true when you are running in a Council race or a race where there are several positions going into the general. Look at your numbers. Even though you won every precinct, you would have won some by a smaller margin. Those are, in reality, your weak precincts. Go out and work them harder. Nothing is guaranteed in politics and your goal is to win every precinct in the general election. You will never do that by thinking that you have it made and don't have to work as hard as your opponents.

You should continue to conduct these phone surveys throughout the campaign going on to the general. You will want to call around fifty "good voters" each time and ask them who they will vote for in the upcoming general election and why they voted for who they did in the primary election. Based on the results, you can see how you're doing and again adjust your strategy. You will also want to call the same batch of fifty voters several weeks apart to see if your strategy is working and if you are gaining support with them. Pick one or two batches of fifty voters for this repeat method of calling.

While I have always used the phone as a survey tool to gauge how my campaign was doing, I have never used what is called a "phone bank." They can be effective, but they can sometimes be difficult to set up, and I have never felt that in my case, they were necessary. If you're running in a large city of a few hundred thousand or more, it may make more sense to use a phone bank. It really boils down to your preference and the amount of money you have to spend. Campaigns can be run in many different ways. Some campaigns will concentrate on using literature more, some may put more emphasis on cable television, some may put more effort into door knocking and some may put a lot of effort into phone banking. It is your personal preference as to how important phone banking is and how much of your resources you want to put into it.

With that being said, here is what phone banking, or GOTV is, and a few ways that you can do it. Phone banking is where you have volunteer supporters working phones, calling the "good voters" on election day and sometimes the day before election day, reminding people to go out and vote and to please support you at the polls. During the campaign, you will end up with a list of supporters who have your sign in their yard and people who have told you that they will support you on election day. These are the people you also want your phone banks to call. Remember to try and get phone numbers of these people as you run into them during the campaign. If you are running in a partisan race, you will want to contact the loyal party voters.

You can do phone banking by having people do it from their homes. Just split up the list of names and numbers and give each person so many people to call. If you are lucky and know someone like a real estate agent who has an office set up with a few dozen phone lines that will let you use them for this, it will make it easier to coordinate. If you have a campaign office set up and you have enough funds to have several phone lines installed, that's the place to do it. However, most people who run for local office generally do not have enough funds for a campaign office.

It doesn't really matter how you do it, the people who receive the calls will never know whether you are calling from a home, campaign office or other office, so it won't matter anyway. The real decision for you to make is whether or not to use phone banking. I don't personally know of many local candidates who use phone banks, but most of the candidates I know, use the phone as a survey tool.

Let's discuss for a minute whether or not to have a campaign office. If you're running in a small or average size community, I would not recommend having a campaign office. You would have to pay rent, make sure someone is there to staff it, and there are a lot of other expenses that go along with a campaign office, such as utility bills, phone installation and bills, etc. You probably will not have enough money to do it. In most cases, you can use your home as your campaign office. Have an extra phone line put in your house and get an answering machine set up. You can have your meetings there and save your money for the more important things like literature, postage, yard signs, etc.

If you are running in a large city, you are going to have more volunteers and materials than you can fit in your home, basement or garage, and so you may need a central campaign office, and you will probably have the funds necessary to set one up. This will give you a central place for your volunteers and a place to store your materials. If you have a commercial campaign office, spend the money for a good alarm system. It wouldn't be the first time that one was broken into and all the yard signs and materials suddenly vanished. If that happens, it will probably be close to the general election when you don't have enough time to replace the materials. Also, if you open a commercial campaign office, you should hire an office manager who will schedule and coordinate staffing for the office. Yes, you can use a volunteer for this, but if you can afford to pay for an office manager, it's worth it. I don't recommend paying for other volunteer workers unless you really feel that you have to.

Chapter Fourteen

On to the General Election

Now that you have won the primary, and of course, we are also going to assume that you are going to win the general election, you might be sitting around at the end of the primary election party wondering what to do next? You already have the answer! The fact that you have made it through the primary means that you have already satisfactorily performed all of the things that you will need to do in the general election. You already **know** the answer and it's simple. You just continue doing exactly what you have been doing the last several months. You will have to continue door knocking, mailing out literature, putting up more yard signs, going to debates and candidate forums, etc. I will go into more of that in a minute, but let's talk about fund raising for the general election.

Now that you have won the primary, you are ten times the viable candidate you were the day before the primary. You have established yourself as an effective campaigner and someone who knows how to win. You have also been accepted well by the voters, which means they like your message, which is why you **do not** change it. You will now have more volunteers than before since some candidates have been weeded out of the race. Of course, now you will need more funds to run your campaign and the good news is that your ability to raise money just increased dramatically, and if you are not smart enough to use that ability to raise money, then you should not have gotten this far in the first place. If there were other candidates running in your race that didn't make it through the primary, their supporters will be looking for someone to support, both financially and otherwise. That someone could very likely be you. Make sure that you capitalize on that by inviting them to your next fund raiser. You need to schedule a fund raiser right away and up the amount you charge for it. Depending on the size of your community and the office that you are running for, you may want to hold two or more fund raisers before the general election, and you need to schedule the first one immediately since you generally only have about seven weeks between the primary and the general elections, and it could even be less time than that. Again, schedule it right away while everyone is still excited and talking about your victory in the primary.

This is very important! **Keep the plan and message the same!** Do not change your tactics for the general. If you do, you may be courting disaster. Some voters might just think that the person they voted for has dropped out of the race and that you are a new person they have never heard of before. You should keep your message the same, and continue to do all of the same things that you did in the primary. The only difference is there are now less candidates in the race!

The only adjustments that you want to make in your overall strategy, other than the neat tip I will explain at the end of this chapter, will be based on the primary precinct results. You will want to go door knocking yourself as the candidate, in the precincts you did poor in. You will also want to do an extra mailing to the precincts you did poor in. Your literature should basically stay the same. You can change the format a little but I recommend staying with the same colors. Maybe you can add a third color to spice it up a little. The important thing is to keep the content the same. Stick with the same issues that got you through the primary. I have seen candidates win the primary and then totally change their issues and strategy! Some of them were not in office after general election day.

Now is when you and your inner circle need to discuss other forms of advertising. The first one to discuss is the use of cable television. As I said earlier, if you have the money, use cable. The best use is the half-hour or hour-long programs where you are being interviewed by someone that you have selected. Also, as I said earlier, unless you have a lot of extra funds, regular television is not worth it. Even in the larger cities, cable can be just as effective and much more reasonable. Radio advertising is generally not worth the price. I have never used radio and it was only because I never could negotiate a good price for the air time. I would have one of your people call the local radio stations and try to negotiate a price, but you will probably find that you will pay less for a thirty-second commercial on cable than on radio.

I used billboards only once, and it was in my last reelection. The rates on billboards vary greatly depending on their location and size. In most cases, they will not be worth the price unless you have a lot of money, but it is worth checking into. If you are running for office in a very large city, you may <u>need</u> to use billboards, but if that is the case, you should be able to afford them. The larger the city, the more money you can raise. If you consider using them, you will have to plan ahead since many of them are already reserved as much as a year in advance. Hopefully, you have followed my advice and read this book from cover to cover before you began, because if you waited to check on billboards until after you won the primary, you probably will not get one. There is another risk with using billboards. You will probably have to put some money down on the billboard before the primary and you may not get that money back if you lose the primary and cancel the billboard. Hey, no one told you it would be easy.

The tough debates are going to happen now before the general election. Get prepared and when you think you are ready, get prepared! I can guarantee you that no matter how much you think you are ready, someone is going to ask you something at the debate that will throw you completely off base. The only thing that will save you is being prepared as best you can, and if you are, you can probably "dance" around the question and give an answer on something entirely different. That's a common tactic used by experienced debaters to make use of their allotted time. Let's say, for instance, someone at the debate asks you the question, "I heard that you support capital punishment, is that true, and if so, why do you think it's okay to take someone's life"? First, since this is a local election, the issue is moot. No one at the local level makes any

105

of those decisions, but they have the right to ask you almost any question during a debate. The question is simply designed to make you squirm. The mistake you could easily make is to spend your entire two or three minutes explaining your position on capital punishment, why you may or may not think it's okay in some cases, and during all this time, you will be uncomfortable with giving the answer. I have seen some candidates go completely off track over one question and never regain their footing again. The people at home (if televised) or in the audience will wonder why the heck this is even being discussed. Don't fall for that. The first five seconds of your answer should be, "That's not really a local issue, and I want to talk about what's important to our community, like taxes and service and issues like that." Then, with your remaining two or three minutes, and without missing a heartbeat, you can continue with something like, "Speaking of taxes, let me explain how I plan to cut the local tax rate by ten percent over the next two years...blah blah blah." Now you have taken a question that was designed to distract you and you have used your allotted time to show the voters that you are concerned with the tax rates in your community. Believe me when I tell you, the listeners will forget all about capital punishment as soon as you start talking about an issue that hits home with them. These are some of the things I spoke about earlier regarding preparation and practice for debates. Don't get caught off guard and don't let them see you sweat!

You will also need to be prepared for the last nasty piece of literature that your opponent or opponents may or may not drop in the last few days of the campaign. These are traditionally called the *"midnight flyers."* It will say something very nasty about you that will not be true, but they will say it anyway since you will not be able to respond in time. The good news is that most of the voters are smarter than people give them credit for and they discount most of these nasty last-minute flyers. They don't like it, and many times, they will do exactly the opposite and vote for you just because of the nasty thing your opponent has done. Remember, America has always had a love affair with the underdog. I would recommend that if you suspect that your opponent may resort to this type of tactic, that you try to preempt him or her by placing a small notice in your last piece of literature that says something like this, "I have heard that my opponent may try some last-minute piece of nasty literature to hurt my chances with the voters. I am banking on the fact that our residents here in our community are more intelligent and professional than to fall for that type of campaigning, and I promise you that I will not resort to this type of nasty campaigning. I do not believe it's good for you or me or the community as a whole. I have too much respect for our residents to resort to using these types of campaign tactics. Let's hope it's just a rumor and thanks for all your support"! This should take care of the problem whether it happens or not. If it does happen, you have predicted it and already told the voters that you will take the positive approach to the election showing respect for the voters. If it does not happen, you have only warned that you heard it may happen, and you still look good in the eyes of the voters since you still promised to stay positive during the election. Whatever happens, the voters will look at you in a positive light.

The local newspapers will again do candidate interviews and do a write-up a few weeks before the general election. They will also do endorsements of candidates for all local offices a week or so before the election. As I said earlier, if they endorse you, you may want to make up some flyers and get a bunch of kids together and drop them door to door in as much of your community as you can, since you most likely will not have enough time to mail them.

Here's the tip I spoke of at the beginning of this chapter. During my first campaign, I was certain that my opponent would beat us in the absentee vote count. He was the incumbent Mayor, and incumbents usually win the absentee votes. The reason is simple. Incumbents always get to interact with the seniors in the community quite often, and usually in a positive manner. Incumbents get to serve food to the seniors at picnics and parties, and sometimes even sponsor or throw picnics for seniors. Remember, seniors often make up the majority of the absentee voters. And, absentee votes can be as much as ten or twenty percent of the total votes cast in any election, so you can see the importance of garnering support from the absentee voters.

So, knowing that my opponent had the edge over me in the absentee votes, I had to come up with some strategy that would offset his advantage. The strategy that I came up with worked fantastic. Here it is. Just a few days before the absentee ballots went out to all the absentee voters, I put together ten teams of two people each. I selected my best workers who knew how to go door knocking and talk to people. I split up the absentee voter list into ten packages of equal numbers and gave a package to each of the ten teams. I had each team go out in a car, one person to drive and keep the car running while the other gets out and runs up to the door to knock. The teams actually drove to each of the homes where the absentee voters lived and knocked on the door and asked the absentee voter to support me in the election. My volunteer explained to the absentee voter that they would be getting their absentee ballot very soon and asked that they mark the ballot for candidate Thomas as their Mayor. What surprised us was that the people seemed delighted to see us! They seemed to feel that since someone would go to all this effort of putting two people in a car and drive to their home just to ask for their support, that their vote really did matter, and really **did** count. All ten teams reported very positive comments from all the voters they visited. For those who were not home, we left them a special letter addressed to them as an absentee voter informing them that they would receive their absentee ballot within a few days and asking them to mark Thomas for Mayor when they filled it out.

Timing is critical here. You can't go out too soon or your opponent will hear about it and attempt to duplicate what you did. You have to go out just a few days before the ballots go out. Most voters will fill out the ballot right away and send it back. If your opponent hears about your special visit, and sends out his volunteers, the odds are that many of the ballots will already be in the mail, filled out. This is exactly why I didn't use this tactic in the primary election. If I had, my opponent would have used this strategy in the general and I would have lost my advantage. I recommend you wait until the general election to use this tactic.

We had no way of knowing for sure how well this tactic worked until election day. When we saw the results, we were elated. All the numbers were up on the vote count board from all the precincts and we had a mere two hundred vote lead. I had told all my workers that we needed at least a three hundred point lead before the absentee votes were counted to have a chance of winning. I felt that my opponent, based on the primary results in the absentee votes, would win the absentee votes in the general. When the votes went up, they were almost even in each of the three absentee precincts and we actually won one of the precincts by a few votes. When it was all over, we kept our two hundred point lead, and won the election! Everyone was shocked that we did so well in the absentee vote, and believe it or not, no one really knew why or how we did it. It was the subject of discussion for the evening and for the next several weeks following the election. This is a great strategy and it really works. All you have to hope for is that your opponent hasn't bought this book yet!

Chapter Fifteen

General Election Day

You will need to prepare for the big day, the day of the general election. You will need to do exactly the same as you did for the primary, only in a larger fashion. You will probably need a larger space. You may want to order some food like pizza or have someone make up some sandwiches or meat and cheese trays to go along with the chips and pretzels. After all, you're in the big time now!

You will need to line up your poll workers for the general election. Again, you will need to decide how many to use, and whether or not to use them if your opponent doesn't. My recommendation for the general election is that if you have the volunteers to use, go ahead and use them at the polls even if your opponent doesn't. You should have enough volunteers by now, especially after winning the primary election. If, however, you're short on volunteers and your opponent doesn't use poll workers, you may want to consider only having workers go to the polls at the closing just to get the number of votes cast for each candidate. You can even have some people stationed at the Clerk's office to get the results and relay them back to you. Make up a blank sheet for your workers to put the numbers on. If you have poll workers out most of the day, you will again need coffee wagons. Unlike the general election eve party, which should be nicer, keep the coffee wagons simple like before. Don't add to the menu just because it's the general election. Tell your coffee wagon workers to give out coffee and food to anyone, even your opponent's workers. This is traditional and professional courtesy. You will find that most coffee wagons operate that way. After all, the election is almost over and everyone should just enjoy the day, get along, and wait for the results. Of course, this doesn't always happen and some poll workers get really nasty. Just make sure that your people stay positive and polite. Everyone will feel better about it after it's all over.

You will need another vote count board, the same as the one you had for the primary, although it should be smaller now, since there will be less candidates. Hang them on a wall high enough so that people can see them over the people standing around in front. If you are in a rental hall, see if they will let you put some long folding tables against the wall and someone can walk on the tables and write in the numbers. If not, use a stepladder. This way, they will be high enough for everyone to see.

You also need to ask the Clerk about the procedure to allow you to have a person who will witness the opening and counting of the absentee ballots. You will want to do this in both the primary and the general election. In most communities, each candidate has the right to have a representative sit in and watch the opening of the absentee ballots to make sure that everything is done properly. I would recommend that you do this in both the primary and the general election.

On general election day, you will want to go around and visit the polling precincts. Stop at each one of them at least twice if you can. You don't have to stay at each one very long, just enough to be seen by the neighbors in that area and to shake a few hands of voters as they go in to vote. Some candidates spend hours at one precinct, but I would recommend that you bounce around from precinct to precinct. If it's a large precinct, you can stay a little longer, but do not spend a long time at a small precinct since it will not be good use of your time.

Make sure that you go home and freshen up before you go to the place where you are going to have your election eve party and watch the final results come in. Get there early so that you can greet everyone who comes to share in your victory, and also to make sure that everything is set up the way you wanted it. As soon as the first numbers

111

begin to come in, make sure that you have the people who you want next to or right around you in place, because if the numbers are in your favor when they come in, you will be crowded by a lot of happy people who will want to put their arm around you and shake your hand. When that starts, your loved ones will not be able to get to you until it settles down, which may be quite awhile. This is a happy event in your life; don't spoil it by not having your loved ones next to you! This is one of those precious moments that only come once and you will regret it if you don't share it with the appropriate loved ones.

Of course, good candidates are always prepared, so you should have written down both speeches: the one for if you lose, and the one you will use if you win. As always, we are planning on you winning, so after you are declared a winner, you will go to the podium and make your victory speech. Try to make sure that you do not make some of the most common mistakes many candidates make. To do this, you will need to write some notes down a few days before...like who to thank, supporters, family, friends, co-workers, etc. Try not to leave anyone out. Also, make sure that your family and loved ones are up at the podium behind you; they deserve it after putting up with everything a campaign throws at them. Have your campaign manager and your inner circle up at the podium also, while you are speaking. Be prepared. It is important to say everything you want to say. This moment in history will only come once; you do not get a second chance, so don't screw it up by not being prepared with some notes as to what you want to say. Also, make sure that someone is taking some pictures and video, you will want it for your scrapbooks and memorabilia collection.

Make your speech a positive one whether it is a concession speech or a victory speech. If it's a victory speech, and we are going to assume that it is, you do not need to run down your opponent, believe me, he or she feels bad enough right about now. Besides, you will gain more respect from everyone by thanking him or her for the great competition and wishing them well. It is tradition for the losing candidate to go to the victory party of the winner and congratulate the winner. This doesn't always happen, but if it does, treat your opponent with the utmost respect and tell all of your volunteers and guests at the party to do the same. Remember, you are the incumbent now and you might as well start acting like one. Besides, think about how you would feel and how you would want to be treated if you were in the same position as them. If your opponent does not come over to congratulate you, don't lose any sleep over it and don't let it spoil your party. He or she will most likely contact you in the next day or so to congratulate you.

This will be one of the greatest moments of your life and a great night for you and your family and you should celebrate it to the fullest. Savor every moment, take lots of pictures and enjoy it because you have some of the most challenging and hard work ahead of you. Being an elected official is not easy and is sometimes thankless work. Some communities will have the winning candidates take over almost immediately and some will have a transition time of several weeks. If you have transition time before you take office, use it wisely to get up to speed on what you need to know to prepare for your new job. If you're lucky, the outgoing incumbent will be willing to bring you up to speed and help you get started. I hope you will enjoy public service as much as I have. It will be one of the most rewarding experiences in your life. I hope this book has been as helpful as I think it will be and well worth the money you spent on it. Congratulations, and good luck!

It is so easy to forget everything that you will need to do in an election. I have provided a simple checklist below that you can refer to as often as you like to make sure that you stay on track during the campaign.

✓ Talk to family, friends and co-workers.
✓ Consider the *"Good and Bad"* of politics.
✓ Get a feel for the level of support for your candidacy, including monetary support.
✓ Make *your* decision to run or not to run.
✓ Get all the proper paperwork filed with the proper elections division.
✓ Open campaign bank account and appoint your campaign manager and treasurer.
✓ Put together your *inner circle.*
✓ Formulate your committees such as fundraising, signs, literature, door knocking, etc.
✓ Put together your campaign volunteer list.
✓ Design your literature and signs.
✓ Make sure that you file the proper election cycle financial reports.
✓ Decide what media advertising you will do, such as cable, television and radio.
✓ Appoint someone to set up your database in the computer and get it set up *early.*
✓ Decide what endorsements you will seek.
✓ Decide what appearance you will make.
✓ Set up a committee to handle any debates and to *prepare you* for the debates, if any.
✓ Make sure that *you* get out in the neighborhoods, knocking on doors and talking with people.
✓ Have a committee set up the election returns party for both the primary and general elections.

Order Form

Fax orders (fax this form)   (734) 454-0557

On-line orders   Order at winelect.com

E-mail us @   mayorwest@winelect.com

Postal orders (mail this form)   R&T Enterprise, Inc.
                                            7474 N. Hix Road
                                            Westland, MI 48185

Quantity
_____   How to Run for Local Office @ $19.95 ea. $ _____
            Michigan residents add 6% sales tax $ _____
            Shipping is $3.00 for the first book; $ _____
            $2.00 for each additional book $ _____
            Total amount enclosed $ _____

Name _____
Street address _____
City_____ State _____ Zip _____
Phone _____ Fax _____
E-mail address_____

Payment Visa_____ MasterCard _____ Check _____ Payable to R&T
                                                  Enterprise, Inc.
Please print name on card _____
Card number _____ Exp. date _____
Cardholder's signature _____